Paul Higgins

Nobody Will Ever Forgive Us

Methuen Drama

Methuen Drama

1 3 5 7 9 10 8 6 4 2

Methuen Drama
A & C Black Publishers Limited
36 Soho Square
London W1D 3QY
www.methuendrama.com

Copyright © 2008 by Paul Higgins

Paul Higgins has asserted his rights
under the Copyright, Designs and Patents Act 1988
to be identified as the author of this work

ISBN 978 1 408 11388 2

A CIP catalogue record for this book
is available from the British Library

Typeset by Country Setting, Kingsdown, Kent
Printed and bound in Great Britain by
Cox & Wyman Ltd, Reading, Berkshire

Nobody Will Ever Forgive Us
By Paul Higgins

First performance at the Traverse Theatre, Edinburgh
21st November 2008

Cast

Johnny	Ryan Fletcher
Dad	Gary Lewis
Cath	Carmen Pieraccini
Mum	Susan Vidler
Patrick	John Wark

Writer	Paul Higgins
Director	John Tiffany
Assistant Director	Joe Douglas
Designer	Naomi Wilkinson
Lighting Designer	Lizzie Powell
Company Stage Manager	Suzie Normand
Deputy Stage Manager	Sunita Hinduja
Assistant Stage Manager	Jenny Raith
Wardrobe Supervisor	Aileen Sherry
Wardrobe Assistant	Katy Lonsdale

CAST BIOGRAPHIES

Ryan Fletcher

Ryan trained at the Royal Scottish Academy of Music and Drama.

Theatre work includes *Cockroach* (National Theatre of Scotland/Traverse Theatre), *365* (National Theatre of Scotland/Edinburgh International Festival), *Black Watch* (National Theatre of Scotland), *The Wolves in the Walls* (National Theatre of Scotland/Improbable), *An Advert for the Army* and *Ae Fond Kiss* (Òran Mór).

Film and television work includes *Taggart, Filthy Rich, River City, The Night Sweeper* and *Stop, Look, Listen.*

Gary Lewis

Theatre work includes *Love Lies Bleeding, One Flew Over The Cuckoo's Nest, Ecstasy, The Conquest of the South Pole , Wasted* (Raindog Theatre Company), *One, Two, Hey!* (Soundhouse), *Aalst* (National Theatre of Scotland/Victoria, Belgium/Tramway, Glasgow), *Brothers of the Brush* (Wiseguise Theatre Company), *The Shepherd's Play* (Glasgow Steiner School), *Billy Connelly Double Bill* (Borderline Theatre), *The Grapes of Wrath* (7:84 Theatre Company), *The Birthday Party* (Arches Theatre), *Snow White* (Tron Theatre), *10 Days In May* (Workers' City), *Freddy Anderson's Krassivy: The Story of John MacLean* and *Rafferty's Cafe.*

Television work includes *Taggart, Wired, Silent Witness, City of Vice, Rehab, Prime Suspect 7, Super Volcano, Rebus, Gunpowder, Treason and Plot* and *The Many Trials of One Jane Doe.*

Film work includes *Valhallah Rising, Farewell, Wasted, Dorothy Mills, Yes, Gangs Of New York, Solid Air, One Life Stand, Billy Elliot, Orphans, Carla's Song, My Name Is Joe, Yasmin, Ae Fond Kiss, True North, The Escapist, Pure, Niceland, Skaggerak, Joyeux Noel, Eragon, The Rocket Post, Cargo, Goal!, Boudica, The Match, Gregory's 2 Girls, Blessed* and *What Where – The Beckett Project.*

Documentary includes *Dungavel* and *Monster of the Glen* (Camcorder Guerillas).

Gary has also recorded numerous dramas for BBC Radio.

Carmen Pieraccini

Carmen trained at the Royal Scottish Academy of Music and Drama.

Theatre work includes *An Advert For The Army, The Way of the World* (Òran Mór), *The Recovery Position* (National Theatre of Scotland Young Company), *Falling* (Poorboy/National Theatre of Scotland), *Boston Marriage* (Rapture Theatre Company), *Jack* and the Beanstalk, *Love Freaks* (Tron Theatre), *Puss In Boots* (Hopscotch Theatre Company), *Losing Alec* and *Like A Virgin* (Cumbernauld Theatre Company).

Television work includes *Dear Green Place, River City, The Key, Brotherly Love, Glasgow Kiss, Taggart* and *G-Force*.

Film work includes *Solid Air, Late Night Shopping, My Life So Far* and *Small Faces*.

Susan Vidler
Theatre work includes *Petrol Jesus Nightmare #5 (In the Time of the Messiah)* (Traverse Theatre, for which she won Best Actress at the Kosovo International Festival 2006), *A Thousand Yards* (Southwark Playhouse), *The Juju Girl* (Traverse Theatre), *Sabina, Trainspotting, The Present* (Bush Theatre), *Trainspotting* (Citizens' Theatre, Glasgow/Traverse Theatre), *Heartless* (ICA London) and *A Better Day* (Theatre Royal Stratford East).

Television work includes *Hustle, Stacked, Rebus, The Last Detective, England Expects, Terry McIntyre, Impact, Love in the 21st Century, The Jump, Kavanagh QC, The Woman In White, Macbeth on the Estate, Stone Cold, Flowers of the Forest, Cracker* and *A Dark Adapted Eye*.

Film work includes *Fallout, Voices From Afar, Poppies, Wilbur Wants To Kill Himself, The Present, Alone, Baby Blue, Trainspotting* and *Naked*.

John Wark
John trained at the Royal Academy of Dramatic Art.

Theatre work includes *The Only Girl In The World* (Fractured Venus/Arcola Theatre), *Jamie The Saxt* (Finborough Theatre), *Tamburlaine* (Bristol Old Vic/Barbican), *Dog In The Manger, Pedro The Great Pretender, Tamar's Revenge* (Royal Shakespeare Company), *The Winter Guest* (Almeida Theatre) and *Torch Song Trilogy* (Tron Theatre).

Television work includes *Robin Hood, The Ten Commandments, Taggart, Nobody Tells Me What To Do* and *G-Force*.

Film work includes *The Oxford Murders, Breaking the Waves, Late Night Shopping, The Night Sweeper, A Curry To Die For* and *Tarantino Connection*.

John has also written and directed the short films *Tamar's Revenge, Some Days It Happens, Deeper, Darker, Still* and *Glasses of Wine*.

CREATIVE TEAM BIOGRAPHIES

Joe Douglas Assistant Director
Joe trained at Rose Bruford College, graduating with a BA (Hons) in Directing.
He is currently working with the National Theatre of Scotland and is supported by the
Mackintosh Foundation under the ITV Theatre Director Scheme.

Directing credits include *Videotape* (Òran Mór), *One for the Road* and *Fantasy
Football* (Battersea Arts Centre). Joe has also worked as Assistant Director on *365*,
The Bacchae (National Theatre of Scotland /Edinburgh International Festival), *Six
Characters in Search of an Author* (National Theatre of Scotland/Royal Lyceum
Theatre, Edinburgh/Citizens' Theatre, Glasgow), *Intimate Exchanges, If I Were You*
(Stephen Joseph Theatre Company) and *Scenes from the Back of Beyond* (Royal Court
Theatre).

In 2006 he completed a directing placement with the Royal Court Theatre and has
directed and assisted on productions for Youth Music Theatre UK including *The Last
Tango, Manifest, Oh! What A Lovely War, Red Hunter* and *Amy's Wedding.*

Paul Higgins Writer
Nobody Will Ever Forgive Us is Paul's first play. His other writing credits are two short
films, *Peripheral Vision* and *Opera Lovers,* for the BBC2 series *Table Twelve.*

As an actor, theatre work includes *Damascus* (Traverse Theatre), *The Tempest* (Tron
Theatre), *Black Watch* (National Theatre of Scotland), *Paul, An Enemy of the
People, The Hare Trilogy* (National Theatre), *The Cosmonaut's Last Message To The
Woman He Once Loved In The Former Soviet Union* (Donmar Warehouse), *Macbeth,
Conversations After A Burial* (Almeida Theatre), *Measure for Measure* (Royal
Shakespeare Company), *The Golden Ass, A Midsummer Night's Dream* (Shakespeare's
Globe), *Night Songs, American Bagpipes, The Conquest of the South Pole* (Royal
Court), *Buried Alive, The Maiden Stone* (Hampstead Theatre), *The Way of the World,
Romeo and Juliet, The Odd Women, A View from the Bridge* (The Royal Exchange
Theatre), *Macbeth* (English Touring Theatre/Lyric Hammersmith), *The Slab Boys
Trilogy* (Young Vic), *The Lady from the Sea* (Lyric Hammersmith/West Yorkshire
Playhouse), *A Wholly Healthy Glasgow* (Royal Court/The Royal Exchange Theatre)
and *The Birthday Party* (Shared Experience).

Television work includes *Hope Springs, No Holds Bard, Silent Witness, The Last
Enemy, The Thick Of It, Low Winter Sun, Murder, Staying Alive, Doctor Finlay,
Tumbledown, A Very Peculiar Practice, A Wholly Healthy Glasgow* and *The Negotiator.*

Film work includes *In The Loop, Red Road, Complicity* and *Bedrooms and Hallways.*

Lizzie Powell Lighting Designer
Lizzie trained at the London Academy of Music and Dramatic Arts.

Her theatre work includes *Cockroach, The Dogstone* and *Nasty, Brutish and Short* (National Theatre of Scotland/Traverse Theatre), *The Wasp Factory, Jack and the Beanstalk* (Cumbernauld Theatre), *The Wall* (Borderline Theatre), *Great Expectations* (Byre Theatre/Prime Productions), *Rupture, Venus as a Boy* (National Theatre of Scotland Workshop), *Making History* (Ouroborous Productions, Dublin), *Travels With My Aunt* (New Wolsey Theatre), *The Recovery Position, Oedipus* (National Theatre of Scotland Young Company), *Home: Edinburgh* (National Theatre of Scotland), *Father Matthew* (Yew Tree Company/Cork Opera House), *Smallone* (Blood in the Alley Productions), *Drenched* (Boilerhouse, for which she was nominated for Best Design at the Manchester Evening News Awards), *The Night Shift* (Mark Murphy), *Vanity Play* (Fuel Productions), *The Foolish Man* (Grass Market Project, The Roundhouse, London), *Bones* (Mama Quillo/Leicester Haymarket/The Bush Theatre), *How to Kill Your Lover* (Theatre Objektiv), *Second City Trilogy* (Cork Opera House), *Romeo and Juliet* (Blood in the Alley Productions/Cork Opera House), *The Ebony Bird* (Blood in the Alley Productions), *Crave* and *Cowboy Mouth* (Liquid Theatre Company).

Lizzie has assisted lighting designer Rick Fisher on *Billy Elliot* (Victoria Palace Theatre).

In 2004, Lizzie won a bursary from NESTA for Lighting Design.

Lizzie is a director of Blood In The Alley Productions.

John Tiffany Director
John studied Classics and Theatre at the University of Glasgow and is Associate Director (New Work) for the National Theatre of Scotland. Previously, he was Associate Director at Paines Plough and Literary Director at the Traverse Theatre.

Recent work includes *The Bacchae* in a new version by David Greig, *Black Watch* by Gregory Burke, *Elizabeth Gordon Quinn* by Chris Hannan, *Home: Glasgow* (National Theatre of Scotland), *Jerusalem* by Simon Armitage (West Yorkshire Playhouse) and *Las Chicas del Tres y Media Floppies* by Luis Enrique Monasterio (Granero Theatre, Mexico City and Edinburgh Festival Fringe).

Work for Paines Plough includes *If Destroyed True* by Douglas Maxwell, *Mercury Fur* by Philip Ridley, *The Straits by* Gregory Burke (also Off-Broadway). Work for the Traverse includes *Gagarin Way* by Gregory Burke (also National Theatre, West End and world tour), *Abandonment* by Kate Atkinson, *Among Unbroken Hearts* by Henry Adam (also National Theatre), *Perfect Days* by Liz Lochhead (also West End) and *Passing Places* by Stephen Greenhorn.

John has won a clutch of awards in recent years including the Critics' Circle Award for Best Director and a South Bank Show Award for *Black Watch*, Fringe Firsts for *Black Watch*, *Las Chicas del Tres y Media Floppies*, *Gagarin Way* and *Perfect Days*, Herald Angels for *The Straits* and *Black Watch* and Critics' Awards for Theatre in Scotland in 2007 for *Black Watch*.

Naomi Wilkinson Designer
Naomi trained on the Motley Theatre Design Course, London.

Recent credits include *Cockroach, The Dogstone* and *Nasty, Brutish and Short* (National Theatre of Scotland/Traverse Theatre), *Peer Gynt* (Dundee Rep, awarded Best Design by the Critics' Awards for Theatre in Scotland 2008*), Mother Courage and Her Children* (Dundee Rep), *Glacier* (Tilted Dance, Queen Elizabeth Hall, South Bank), *Critical Mass* (Almeida Opera), *Casanova* (West Yorkshire Playhouse/Lyric Theatre Hammersmith), *On Religion* (Soho Theatre) and *A Midsummer Night's Dream* (Dundee Rep, awarded Best Design (with Bruno Poet) by Critics' Awards for Theatre in Scotland 2007).

Other credits include *Just for Show* (DV8 Physical Theatre, National Theatre/ International Tour), *The Misanthrope* (Guildhall School of Music & Drama), *A Family Affair* (Arcola Theatre), *Don't Look Back* (Dreamthinkspeak/site-specific/Stanmer House Brighton/Somerset House London, winner of Total Theatre Award Edinburgh 2005), *The Accidental Death of an Anarchist* (Octagon Theatre), *Colder Than Here* (Soho Theatre), *Happy Yet?* (Gate Theatre London), *The Firework-Maker's Daughter*, *I'm a Fool to Want You, A Little Fantasy, Shoot Me in the Heart, I Can't Wake Up, Happy Birthday Mr Deka D, I Weep at My Piano* (Told By An Idiot), *Arcane* (Piano Circus/UK Tour), *Mules, My Life in the Bush of Ghosts, Heredity* (Royal Court Theatre Upstairs) and *Two Horsemen* (Gate Theatre).

NATIONAL THEATRE OF SCOTLAND

The National Theatre of Scotland is unique in being building-free. This innovative model means that we are able to perform in a huge variety of theatres, halls and found spaces. Equally importantly, it allows us the freedom to collaborate with a richly diverse mixture of venues, companies, festivals and individuals to fulfil our key aim of producing world-class theatre for the people of Scotland and beyond.

In our short life to date, we have already produced, co-produced and staged some remarkable pieces of theatre such as **Black Watch, The Bacchae, 365, Tutti Frutti, The Wolves in the Walls**, **The Emperor's New Kilt** and **Aalst**. However, we will never be content simply to celebrate past success and are always looking to the future.

In Autumn 2008, we co-produced with the Traverse Theatre, Edinburgh a season of new writing, **Debuts: Cockroach** by Sam Holcroft, directed by National Theatre of Scotland Artistic Director Vicky Featherstone, **The Dogstone** by Kenny Lindsay and **Nasty, Brutish and Short** by Andy Duffy, both directed by Dominic Hill, Artistic Director of the Traverse and **Nobody Will Ever Forgive Us** by Paul Higgins, directed by John Tiffany, National Theatre of Scotland Associate Director for New Work.

For the latest information on all of our activities visit our online home at **www.nationaltheatrescotland.com**

NATIONAL THEATRE OF SCOTLAND

THE TRAVERSE
Artistic Director Dominic Hill

The importance of the Traverse is difficult to overestimate . . . without the theatre, it is difficult to imagine Scottish playwriting at all. (Sunday Times)

The Traverse's commissioning process embraces a spirit of innovation and risk-taking that has launched the careers of many of Scotland's best-known writers including John Byrne, David Greig, David Harrower and Liz Lochhead. It is unique in Scotland in that it fulfils the crucial role of providing the infrastructure, professional support and expertise to ensure the development of a dynamic theatre culture for Scotland.

The Traverse Theatre, the festival's most prestigious home of serious drama.
(New York Times)

From its conception in the 1960s, the Traverse has remained a pivotal venue in Edinburgh. It receives enormous critical and audience acclaim for its programming, as well as regularly winning awards. Most recently, Alan Wilkins' commission for the Traverse, *Carthage Must Be Destroyed,* won Best New Play at the 2008 Critics' Awards for Theatre in Scotland. From 2001–07, Traverse productions of *Gagarin Way* by Gregory Burke, *Outlying Islands* by David Greig, *Iron* by Rona Munro, *The People Next Door* by Henry Adam, *Shimmer* by Linda McLean, *When the Bulbul Stopped Singing* by Raja Shehadeh, *East Coast Chicken Supper* by Martin J Taylor, *Strawberries in January* by Evelyne de la Chenelière in a version by Rona Munro and *Damascus* by David Greig have won Fringe First or Herald Angel awards (and occasionally both). In 2008 the Traverse's Festival programme *Manifesto* picked up an incredible sixteen awards including a record seven Scotsman Fringe Firsts and four Herald Angels.

A Rolls-Royce machine for promoting new Scottish drama across Europe and beyond.
(The Scotsman)

The Traverse's success isn't limited to the Edinburgh stage. Since 2001, Traverse productions of *Gagarin Way, Outlying Islands, Iron, The People Next Door, When the Bulbul Stopped Singing, The Slab Boys Trilogy, Mr Placebo* and *Helmet* have toured not only within Scotland and the UK, but in Sweden, Norway, the Balkans, Germany, USA, Iran, Jordan and Canada. Immediately following the 2006 Edinburgh Festival, the Traverse's production of *Petrol Jesus Nightmare #5 (In the Time of the Messiah)* by Henry Adam was invited to perform at the International Festival in Priština, Kosovo and won the Jury Special Award for Production. During spring 2008, the Traverse toured its award-winning 2007 production of *Damascus* to Toronto, New York and Moscow.

Discover more about the Traverse at www.traverse.co.uk

TRAVERSE THEATRE

Nobody Will Ever Forgive Us

To Amelia

Characters

Johnny, *twenty-two*
Patrick, *nineteen*
Cath, *eighteen*
Mum, *forty-one*
Dad, *forty-two*

1 Thursday Night

The sitting room of a tenement flat.

Johnny *is searching for money. He looks a bit rough. He looks under the rug, the couch, an ornament. He's looked in all these places before. His search becomes steadily more ridiculous.*

He stares at the large sideboard. He checks his watch. He opens one half of the sideboard, then quickly closes it again. He opens the other half, pokes about gingerly, then hauls the contents onto the floor. He rummages. Nothing.

He exits to the kitchen. We hear him rummaging.

Patrick *enters wearing a grey V-neck jumper, a white shirt and grey school-type trousers. He is carrying a cheap suitcase.*

Johnny *re-enters necking a half-bottle of gin.*

Johnny   Jesus! I didn't hear you come in.

Patrick   Sorry.

Johnny   What're you doing here?

Patrick   I live here.

Johnny   Aye, now, I mean.

Patrick   It's the holidays.

Johnny   Have you got any money on you?

Patrick   No. Sorry.

Johnny   Nothing?

Patrick   No.

Johnny   Do men of the cloth not carry money?

Patrick   I'm not a man of the cloth.

Johnny *(offering the bottle)*   Do you want a drink?

Patrick   Get a bottle of tonic and we can take turns.

Johnny   They teaching you to be funny at the seminary?

Patrick   No.

Johnny   I thought not.

He starts to refill the sideboard.

Tam Burnett gave me a cast-iron tip for the dogs and I can't get anything on it. Fourteen to one. The race is in twenty minutes.

Patrick   What's a cast-iron tip when it's at home?

Johnny   Tam knows what he's talking about. He knows a guy who *really* knows what he's talking about. Can you not lend me thirty quid?

Patrick   I haven't got thirty quid.

Johnny   I'll pay you back forty.

Patrick   What if it loses?

Johnny   I'll still pay you back forty.

Patrick   Where are you going to get forty quid if you can't scrape thirty together?

Johnny   Never you mind how. I will.

Patrick   You sound like Dad.

Johnny   Aye, well, you sound like Mum. Lend me a tenner then.

Patrick   I haven't got a tenner.

Johnny   Come on, you must have.

Patrick   Well, how come you haven't?

Johnny   Eh?

Patrick   If I must have a tenner, how come you haven't got one?

They hear the front door opening.

Johnny   Shit!

He puts the gin back in the kitchen.

Mum *and* **Cath** *enter.* **Cath** *has bad eczema in the folds of her skin which she rakes periodically.*

Mum   What happened?

Patrick   When?

Mum   Why are you here?

Patrick   It's the holidays.

Mum   My God. I thought someone had died.

Patrick   Who?

Mum   I don't know. One of the priests.

Patrick   What would I be doing here if one of the priests had died?

Mum   I don't know. (*Indicating sideboard.*) What are you looking for?

Patrick   I'm not. Johnny was –

Johnny *enters from kitchen.*

Johnny   I was looking for that old *Wishaw Press* with the photo of the school team.

Mum   What for?

Johnny   Pat wanted to see it.

Mum   What did you want to see that for?

Patrick   I was trying to remember what Johnny looked like without a pot belly.

Johnny   Aye, very good. He wanted to see what a half-decent footballer looks like.

Patrick   What, is Mick Logan *in* that picture?

Johnny   Mick Logan? I was twice the player Mick Logan was. If it wasn't for my knee.

Mum   And your total lack of application.

Johnny   Aye, let's all tear into me, why don't we? Now that Father Patrick has graced us with his presence. Let's rip into Johnny boy.

Mum   I thought it was next week, your holidays.

Patrick   They decided to let us home early. The exams are finished. We were just hanging around.

Mum   How did you get on?

Patrick   Fine, I think.

Johnny   Will it be straight As again, Your Holiness?

Patrick   I expect so, Johnny, what can I say?

Johnny   How about 'Let's wait for the results'? Eh? Or have they made you infallible early?

Cath   Don't start, the pair of you.

Cath *is scratching behind her knee.*

Patrick   How's your skin?

Cath   Terrible.

Mum   We were at the dermatologist earlier on. (*Admonishing her.*) He says she has to be patient, and not get so stressed. And stop scratching!

Cath   It's my one pleasure.

Johnny   Get St Patrick, here, to lay hands on her. That'll sort you out. You can fix my knee while you're at it.

Mum   I haven't even got your bed ready.

Patrick   Don't worry about it.

Mum   Why wasn't I told?

Patrick   They only decided last night.

Mum Why?

Cath (*to* **Mum**) Let's see what Pat thinks.

Mum What?

Cath Let's see what Pat thinks.

Mum Eh? Never mind that.

Patrick What?

Mum Never mind.

Cath Mum and me have had an idea.

Mum Shush! They'll just pour scorn, as usual.

Patrick What?

Mum Here, come and I'll sort your bed out. I'll sleep in here.

Patrick I'm happy sleeping in here.

Mum *tries to pick his case up.*

Patrick I'll get it.

As they exit . . .

Mum What have you got on your feet?

Patrick Where I come from, we call them shoes.

Mum I see you haven't got any funnier . . .

Cath *and* **Johnny** *are alone.*

Cath Have you got it?

Johnny Not yet.

Cath For fuck's sake, Johnny.

Johnny I know. It's coming. Somebody let me down.

Cath We're going in on Saturday. The price goes up on Monday, so I can't put her off again.

Johnny Why's the price going up?

Cath   It's a promotion or something, I don't know.

Johnny   I thought the guy was going to hold it.

Cath   He is, but she has to pay for it before it goes up.

Johnny   Fucking hell.

Cath   You said you would definitely, without fail, on our sister's grave, have it today.

Johnny   I know! I just said! A guy let me down! What about Pat? He must have money.

Cath   Leave Pat out of it. You owe me it, you pay me it back.

Johnny   I'm going to. Uncle Joe slips him fifty quid every time he sees him – 'That's for you, son. Don't tell your mother.' Did you see him at wee Higgy's wedding? He could hardly move for people fucking *forcing* money into his pockets, the jammy bastard.

Cath   Be sure to call him that when you ask him for his dosh.

Johnny   We'd have a better chance if you ask him.

Cath   No way, sunshine. Forget it.

Johnny   He won't lend it to me.

Cath   No, that's right, because he's not as stupid as your fucking idiot sister. His head doesn't zip up the back. I could strangle you. Nobody in our whole family will ever forgive us. Jinty, Jim, Uncle Joe, Auntie Ella, Auntie Pat, Theresa, Kathleen, Bridget . . .

Johnny   I get the picture. I'm going to see somebody later on tonight. I've got an idea. I'll get it. Do you want a drink?

Cath   Of course I want a fucking drink, I can feel my skin cracking up just listening to you.

Johnny (*on his way to the kitchen*)   Vodka and Coke?

Cath   No, just a glass of milk – of course a fucking vodka and Coke. In the can. Pour half the Coke out and top it up – she's nipping my head.

Mum *and* **Patrick** *re-enter with* **Patrick***'s bedding.* **Patrick** *carries a book or two.*

Patrick   I'm happy on the couch and I'm happy with my shoes, OK?

Mum   If you say so.

Johnny (*offstage*)   Anybody else want a drink?

Mum   No.

Patrick   No thanks.

Mum   What are you drinking?

Cath   Just a Coke. Mum and me are thinking of going to a medium.

Mum   You just don't know how to keep your mouth shut, do you?

Cath   What do you think?

Patrick   What for?

Cath   To get our eyes tested, bonedome. Why do you think?

Johnny *enters with a can of lager and a can of 'Coke'.*

Cath   What if it *is* possible to communicate with, you know, if they're just somewhere else? (*To* **Patrick**.) You believe in life after death. So what if we could talk to Ruth and we just sat here not bothering?

Nobody says anything.

I mean, what have we got to lose? If she's there, great, if she isn't . . .

Again, nobody speaks.

Well, say something, for Christ's sake.

Patrick   Eh . . . I'd like to talk to her, too, Cath. I do talk to her, in fact. But I don't expect anything back.

Cath   But what if?

Patrick   I just don't believe in it.

Cath   What if, though? Where's the harm?

Patrick   Well . . . children do die. All the time. Thousands of children die of hunger every day.

Johnny   You've sent him into missionary mode. What's that got to do with Ruth?

Patrick   We have to face the facts.

Mum   I told you it was no use talking to him.

Cath (*to* **Johnny**)   What do you think?

Johnny   Well, I hate to say it but I agree with Pope Paddy there. It's a con. They take advantage of vulnerable people.

Cath   Who are you calling vulnerable?

Patrick   We're all vulnerable. We loved her and we miss her and we'd all like her to walk in the door right now but it's not going to happen . . .

They hear the front door opening.

Dad *walks in. He's forty-two, handsome, stocky, and has a full head of black hair. He's wearing a nondescript suit with an Irn-Bru bottle in the jacket pocket. He's had a few drinks but is in control.*

Johnny   Jesus!

Dad   What?

Johnny   Nothing. We were hoping for someone else.

Dad   Who?

Johnny   Never mind.

Dad   What are you doing here?

Patrick   'Welcome home, son.' I'm on my holidays.

Dad   Your life's one long holiday. (*Indicating* **Johnny**'s *lager.*) I'll have one of them, thanks, since they're mine. And get one for Patrick.

Patrick   I'm OK, thanks.

Johnny *goes to the kitchen.*

Mum *(as cold as she can be, throughout)*   Don't you think you've had enough?

Dad   Not by a long chalk.

Mum   Where have you been?

Dad   Where have I been?

Mum   Where have you been. You were supposed to be back here at eleven o'clock this morning.

She checks her watch.

Ten hours ago.

Dad   I had to see somebody about a job.

Mum   In the pub?

Dad   Aye in the pub, now give us peace.

He goes to sit.

Mum   Hand it over.

Dad   Hand what over?

Mum   You know very well what.

Dad   Do I?

Mum   I've got no money to feed these children till Saturday.

Johnny *returns with* **Dad***'s lager, then sits down to read the* Daily Record.

Dad   They're old enough and ugly enough to feed themselves. Thanks, son.

Mum   Catherine has paid her digs, she's entitled to her dinner.

Dad   Is that right? And what about Johnny boy?

Mum   He's owing me it.

Dad Aye, well, owe him his dinner, then.

Johnny I'm not hungry.

Dad And what about young Patrick there? Where's his contribution?

Mum Don't you dare. He's just this minute walked in the door. It's *your* digs I'm after.

Dad My digs?

Mum Your digs.

Dad And why would I pay digs in my own house? Tell me that. Who pays the rent, I'd like to know?

Mum The social security pays the rent.

Dad Aye, on my behalf.

Mum Don't make me laugh.

Dad You can laugh all you want. You can laugh till you're blue in the face, for all I care. Twenty-five years I've worked. Twenty-five years I've paid my stamp. I'm entitled to everything I get, now, and more.

Mum Well, do you think the social security might do some shopping on your behalf? There isn't a scrap of food in the house.

Dad Is that right? Well, don't you worry about that. Don't you worry about that one bit.

Mum Who will?

Dad Nobody. Nobody needs to worry about it because there's nothing to worry about. I'll make sure my children are fed. Don't you worry about that.

Mum How?

Dad How what?

Mum What are you going to feed them with?

Dad   Food, I was thinking of.

Mum   What are you going to buy it with?

Dad   I've got money. Don't you worry about that.

Mum   How much?

Dad   Plenty.

Mum   Let's see it then.

Dad   Aye, very good. I don't need to show you nothing, my friend. Not a single thing. Everything's under control. You leave the fiscal planning to me.

Mum   Oh, you're such a big shot. That's why your son here is wearing someone else's shoes.

Dad   What are you havering about, woman?

Mum   A boy at the seminary had to give Patrick a pair of his shoes.

Dad   What's wrong with your own shoes?

Patrick   They just wore out. I'm perfectly happy with these.

Dad   I'll sort you out a pair tomorrow.

Patrick   I'm happy with these, thanks. More than happy.

Dad   No son of mine wears borrowed shoes.

Mum   It would appear that fifty per cent of them do.

Dad   I'll sort you out a pair tomorrow. And I'll get your pal a pair as well.

Mum   I'd hold on to those for the time being, if I were you.

Dad   I'll have twenty pairs of shoes for you first thing tomorrow.

Mum   One will do.

Dad   Forty top-quality shoes first thing.

Mum   We'll believe it when we see it.

Dad   Oh you'll see it all right, don't you worry about that. I'm in charge of the family finances now. I'll put some decent food into these children. Salad. Steak. Fish. No more crisps and chocolate cups and Irn-Bru. You won't see me running out of money on a Wednesday.

Mum   You wouldn't make it past Saturday night. Buying drinks for all your useless pals, telling each other what great men you are while your children starve.

Dad   Who's starving? Get a grip of yourself.

Mum   Do you know that boy has only got the clothes he's wearing, and two spare shirts? Not a pair of jeans. Not a T-shirt. His case is full of books.

Dad   I'll get you clothes, son. You can have anything you want, money no object. And we're talking top-quality kit here, no rubbish. You too, Cathy.

Mum   You going to get her twenty pairs of shoes as well?

Dad (*ignoring her*)   What do you need, Pat? A couple of suits? Just tell me what you need and I'll sort it. What do you need?

Patrick*'s just noticed there's no telly.*

Dad   Johnny . . . Eh, Pat. What do you need, Pat son?

Patrick   I'm fine. I don't need anything.

Dad   You sure? Because I'll tell you something, and you can ask anybody in this town, *anybody*: what John Conlan says, John Conlan does.

Mum   Aye, but only if he says he's going to the Cross Keys.

Dad (*ignoring her*)   Anything you want, son, just let me know.

Patrick   I'm fine. Where's the telly?

Cath   Good question.

Dad   Shoes . . . suits . . . socks . . . pants . . . shirts . . . ties. Coats. Just say the word. Jeans. Top quality. Do you want a cup of tea?

Mum   Never mind tea, he wants to know where the telly is.

Dad   And how would I know where it is?

Cath (*to* **Patrick**)   It's missing.

Dad   And it can stay missing, as far as I'm concerned. I never so much as glance at it. Apart from Attenborough. It's a matter of complete indifference to me where it is. Do you want a cup of tea, Pat?

Patrick   No, I'm fine, ta.

Dad   Things are going to change in this house. From now on.

Mum   I can't wait.

Dad   You don't need to wait. From this minute. From this second. You go to your bed and leave it to me.

Mum   I'll decide when I go to bed.

Dad   It's a matter of complete indifference to me when you go to bed. You can stay up all night. It's of no concern to me. You can stay up for the rest of your life. The priests have got the right idea, son. Avoid women at all costs, they ruin everything.

Mum   He knows better than to take advice from you. Look at you.

Dad   Nothing wrong with me, hen, not a single solitary thing. I mean it, son, they destroy everything. You'll be watching a right good western, then a woman rides into town and that's it ruined.

Cath   Right, Dad, do you think you could give it a rest? My ears are starting to bleed.

Dad   Is that so? Your ears are starting to bleed, are they? Very good. Eh, Pat? Cath's ears are starting to bleed. What do you make of that?

No reply.

Eh, Pat, son. What do you make of that?

Patrick   What?

Dad   Cath's ears are starting to bleed, what do you make of that?

Patrick   I don't know.

Dad   You don't know? Eh, Johnny, he doesn't know, eh?

Johnny   He doesn't know much.

Dad   And there was me thinking he knew everything.

Johnny   No, that's me.

Patrick   I think it might have been a metaphor.

Dad   A metaphor? It was a metaphor all right. There's no doubt it was a metaphor. Would you concur with that, Johnny boy? That it was metaphorical?

Cath   Dad, I swear, if you don't shut up I'll cut your throat.

Dad   Oh I'll shut up all right. Don't you worry about that. I'll shut *right* up . . . How keener than a serpent's tooth, eh, Johnny? How keener than a serpent's tooth.

Mum   I'm away before the poetry starts. Night-night.

Patrick   Night.

Johnny   Night.

Cath   Night.

Mum (*to* **Cath**)   Don't sit up drinking.

Cath   I won't.

Mum *exits.*

Cath *goes to the kitchen.*

Patrick *sits with his book.*

Dad *takes the Irn Bru bottle from his jacket pocket. It's half full of a muddy-looking liquid that clearly isn't Irn-Bru. He gives it a good shake then takes a slug. Silence. Another slug*

Cath *comes in with a can of lager and another can of 'Coke'.*

Johnny   Ta.

Dad   What's that you're reading?

Patrick   Just a book.

Dad   Aye, I can see it's a book. What book?

Patrick   It's called *Escaping History*.

Dad   *Escaping History*. What's it about?

Patrick   It's hard to explain.

Dad   What kind of book is it? Fiction? Fact? Biography? Thriller?

Patrick   It's sort of . . . advice.

Dad   Advice? Advice for what?

Patrick   Just . . . general . . . You'd have to read it. I'll lend you it.

Dad *has another slug.*

Dad   *Escaping History*. Do they never teach you about real history?

Patrick   It's not a school book.

Dad   The Trade Union movement, eh? A bit of real history? The history of the working man. The General Strike? The Jarrow March? The . . . Martyrs, what do you call them? The . . . something Martyrs . . .

Patrick   The Tolpuddle Martyrs.

Dad   The Tolpuddle Martyrs.

Patrick   Aye.

Dad   That's real history, son. None of your kings and queens. The Second World War. The NHS. Attlee. Bevan. The working man taking control of his destiny. Real politics. From each according to his ability, to each according to his needs.

Patrick   Is that not Marx?

Dad   Same thing, son. The Russian Revolution.

He takes another slug. **Patrick** *sees the strange colour of the liquid.*

Patrick   What's that you're drinking?

Dad   Nothing, son. Just a wee something.

Patrick   Where from?

Dad   Just a guy. (*To* **Johnny**.) Where *is* the telly?

Johnny   I don't know. We've been through this.

Dad   Well, it's nothing to do with me.

Cath   Well, don't look at me.

Silence. **Johnny** *concentrates on his paper.* **Dad** *has another slug.*

Dad   Hey, Pat, do they ever let you watch films in there?

Patrick   Sometimes.

Dad   Have you seen *ET*?

Patrick   No.

Dad   But you know what I'm talking about?

Patrick   It's only fifty miles up the road, you know, it's not on Jupiter.

Dad   How do you know ET's a protestant?

Johnny   I don't know. How?

Dad   Cos he looks like one.

Patrick *laughs, in spite of himself, then goes back to his book.*

Dad   Hey, Pat, you know Funky Feenan?

Patrick   I don't think so.

Dad   You must know Funky. Spends his every waking hour leaning on the railings at the foot of the town. People give directions by him. 'Go down to the foot of the town and turn right at Funky Feenan.'

Patrick   I think I know who you mean.

Dad   You must know him. Face like a sack of chisels. He was up in court yesterday for breach of the peace and the judge said he was *inclined* to give him thirty days and did he have anything to say for himself, and Funky said, 'Yes, Your Honour, you're a wizened-faced old bastard.'

Everyone is amused.

Sixty days he got. 'A wizened-faced old bastard.'

He has another slug.

Aye, turn left at Funky Feenan.

Silence. **Patrick** *and* **Johnny** *read,* **Dad** *and* **Cath** *are lost in their thoughts.*

Dad   You know Gerry McDermott with the two wooden legs, Pat son?

Patrick   Yeah.

Dad   We're in the Cross Keys and Gerry keeps levering himself up and launching into 'Scotland the Brave' every five minutes, getting on everyone's nerves, and Funky says to him, 'Haw, Gerry, if you don't pack that in I'll burn you to the ground.'

Patrick *laughs.*

Dad   Aye, 'I'll burn you to the ground.' What are you reading?

Patrick   I told you.

Another slug.

Dad   You'll never learn anything from a book, son. Take that from me . . . Never learn anything from a book. That's a stone-cold fact . . . A cast-iron certainty.

Slug. Silence.

> 'Season of mists and mellow fruitfulness . . .
> Close bosom-friend of the . . . '

What is it again? . . . Something sun. 'Maturing sun.'

> 'Season of mists and mellow fruitfulness,
> Close bosom-friend of the . . . '

Forgotten again.

Ho ho . . . 'maturing sun.'

Slug. Silence.

> 'Is there for honest poverty that hings his head and a' that?
> The coward slave we pass him by, we dare be poor for a' that.
> For a' that and a' that, our toil's obscure and a' that . . . '

He's losing his way.

> 'A man's a man for a' that . . .
> Yes, a man's a man for a' that.'

Slug.

Eh?

> 'The coward slave we pass him by.'

Slug.

> 'The curfew tolls the knell of parting day,
> The lowing herd winds slowly o'er the lea,
> The ploughman homeward plods his weary way,
> And leaves the world to darkness and to me.'

Slug.

He speaks, as if by Keats, the first five lines of Paul Anka's 'My Way'.

Slug.

(*Indicating the electric fire.*) My heart's as big as that fire . . . Pat,
son.

Patrick *turns to him.*

Dad   My heart's as big as that fire. You ask anybody in
Wishaw. Motherwell and Wishaw. Scotland. As big as that fire.

Patrick *sort of nods then turns back to his book.* **Dad** *has another slug.*

Dad   Go up that street and ask anybody you like.

Another slug.

I'm the greatest man in history. Without a shadow of a doubt.
The greatest man in history.

Another slug.

Silence.

His head falls forward.

Patrick   Do you want to go to bed, Dad?

Dad *is about to drop his bottle.* **Patrick** *leaps up, takes it from him
and puts it on the floor.*

Cath   That's him now till the morning.

Patrick   Dad!

No reply.

He gently shakes **Dad***'s shoulder.*

Patrick   C'mon, I'll help you to bed, Dad.

Dad *just moans.*

Patrick *helps him up and out.*

Cath *has a slug of* **Dad***'s bottle.*

Cath   Tomorrow, or we're in the shit.

Lights.

2   Friday Morning

There's no one in the sitting room.

Patrick'*s crumpled bedding is still on the couch. Last night's clothes are draped over a chair.*

Johnny *enters from outside. He's been out all night. He checks in the kitchen, then quickly searches* **Patrick**'*s things. He has a sip from* **Dad**'*s poteen.*

Patrick *returns from a run, wearing skintight shorts.*

Johnny   What the fuck are you wearing?

Patrick   Running gear.

Johnny   Jesus Christ. Look at the state of you. What's wrong with proper shorts?

Patrick   They are proper shorts.

Johnny   Have you not got any football shorts?

Patrick   Yeah, I wear them when I'm playing football. These are running shorts.

Johnny   You look like a screaming poof. Are you trying to get yourself beaten up?

Patrick   No, I'm trying to stay fit and mind my own business.

Johnny   Well, you look fucking ridiculous.

Patrick   That's a big blow coming from you, Johnny boy, because you look absolutely tip-top. What's your secret? Is there a particular *brand* of cigarette you'd recommend?

Johnny   You're not too old for a slap in the puss, you know.

Patrick   Yes I am.

This is a face-off. After a bit, **Johnny** *laughs, shakes his head and sits down.*

Patrick *goes to the kitchen. We hear him rummaging. He comes back.*

Patrick   What do you have for breakfast these days?

Johnny   Nothing.

Patrick   I'm ravenous.

Johnny   Cut down on the running.

Cath *comes in, dressed for work, with a large tub of E45.*

Cath   Morning.

Patrick   Morning.

She looks meaningfully at **Johnny**, *who shakes his head.*

Cath   What are we going to do?

Johnny *doesn't answer.*

Cath   What are we going to do?

Patrick *looks at them.*

Cath   Tell me!

Johnny *says nothing.*

Patrick   What's up?

Cath   We're in big trouble, Pat.

Patrick   How?

Cath *looks to* **Johnny**.

Johnny   Can you lend me three hundred quid?

Cath   Three hundred and twenty.

Patrick   Eh? What for?

Johnny   What does it matter? I'll pay you back.

Patrick (*to* **Cath**)   What's this about?

Cath   It's a long story.

Patrick *waits for the long story.* **Cath** *looks at* **Johnny**, *then at her watch.*

Cath   You want *me* to tell him?

Johnny   It's up to you.

Patrick   Tell me.

Cath   Johnny got caught stealing money from his work. He'd got himself into debt with some heavy guys playing snooker. He already owed me and Mum and Rosemary money.

Johnny   Right, hang on a minute. At least get your –

Cath   I thought you wanted me to tell him. Do you want to tell him?

Johnny   No, I just wanted to point out in my –

Cath   Well, don't fucking interrupt me then. I don't have time. Forgive my language; it's terrible. So he started stealing from his work and got caught. Can't even fucking steal properly. His manager said he wouldn't call the police if he got someone to bring the money to the shop immediately. Three hundred and twenty pounds. So he phoned me. I didn't have it, so I phoned Elizabeth and she didn't have it, so then I phoned Auntie Jean because I knew she had it, but she wasn't in . . . so, and I'm ashamed, I took it from her holiday account. I've got her card and I knew she wouldn't be needing it for months and Johnny said he would pay it back within the week, so she would never be any the wiser. Otherwise he was going to get a record or even go to jail.

Patrick   Why have you got her card?

Cath   She's scared of cash machines – her pal Sadie got mugged at one, so she used to give me her card to go and get her bingo money, because she always drops in here on her way, and it ended up just being easier for me to keep it. Can I just point out, here, that the reason she trusts me is because I'm one-hundred-fucking-per-cent trustworthy. (*To* **Johnny**.) I could kill you for dragging me into this. (*To* **Patrick**.) Jim Rodgers in Toronto sends her forty pounds a week for her bingo and her holidays, and now I'm supposed to go to the travel agent's with her tomorrow morning to pay for her trip to Lourdes with Sadie. And I haven't got it because that useless lump has broken promise after promise. And now I've got to go to work and I'm at my wits' end.

She's putting on some cream.

Patrick (*to* **Johnny**)   What are you going to do?

Johnny   Can you not lend me it? I'll pay you back.

Patrick   You shouldn't need to say that. *Lend* implies *pay back*. What makes you think I've got that kind of money?

Johnny   Vittorio Montesi gave you the fattest envelope I've ever seen when you did the readings at Christmas. And he hardly knows you – it was like *The Godfather*.

Patrick   You think I kept it?

Johnny   You must have kept some of it.

Patrick   Why?

Johnny   Come on, Uncle Joe gives you money every time you make the sign of the fucking cross.

Cath   Johnny!

Patrick *just looks at* **Johnny**.

Johnny   Sorry. Sign of the cross, sorry.

Patrick   I haven't got it.

Johnny   If you don't want to lend me it, just say so.

Patrick   I'm telling you, I haven't got it.

Johnny   Don't lie to me. Don't insult my intelligence.

Patrick   I'm not lying. I haven't got it.

They look at each other.

Cath   What now, Superman?

Johnny   Are you serious?

Patrick   Deadly serious.

Cath   Well, I am well and truly fucked. Thanks a million, Johnny.

Johnny   No, you're not. I know how I can get it all back and more.

Cath   How?

Johnny   You won't go for it.

Cath   For what?

Johnny   You won't go for it.

Cath   What?

Johnny   Frankie Fisher will take me on at snooker for any amount I care to mention.

Cath   Here we go.

Patrick   Why?

Johnny   Because he's loaded and he reckons he's the best player in the club.

Patrick   And is he?

Johnny   He's the second best.

Cath   So why does he think he's the best?

Johnny   Because he's won the last couple of frames we've played. But it was just casual stuff. Showboating. If I bet him, say, four hundred quid, best of nine, on the tournament table, tomorrow night in front of all the regulars, he'll bite my arm off. And I'll beat him.

Patrick   And where do we get the four hundred?

Johnny   We? What's it to you? It's not your problem.

Patrick   I don't want Cath to get into trouble. And I don't want Auntie Jean upset.

Johnny   She can get it from her work, no bother.

Patrick   Can you?

Cath   Are you actually considering this?

Patrick   I just want to know if it's doable.

Johnny   Mrs Calder keeps a grand in cash in the shop at all times. For when people want to sell their family heirlooms. Cath has the run of the place from Friday lunchtime to Monday afternoon. She lent Rosemary six hundred once.

Cath   Aye, for about fifteen hours. (*To* **Patrick**.) She had to pay for a car and her wages hadn't cleared. She was going to get her dad to drive the cash down from Oban. I saved him the trip. (*To* **Johnny**.) Why don't you ask him?

Johnny   Talk sense.

Patrick   So you could get it?

Cath   I am not risking my job for him. It's bad enough I have to hide the fucking keys from him.

Patrick   But you could, in theory?

Cath   Aye, but only if I can definitely put it back first thing on Monday. She takes her mum up to her place in Ballater at the weekends . . .

She looks at her watch.

I'm going to be late opening up.

Patrick (*to* **Johnny**)   You sure you can beat him?

Johnny   Positive. He's a flash git, can't play safe, can't grind, if I get my head down, tie up the pink and black, get the reds awkward, take my time between shots, I'll slaughter him.

Patrick   What do you think?

Cath   Are you serious? It was snooker that got him into all this trouble in the first place.

Johnny   No, it wasn't, those guys are gangsters. They wouldn't let me walk away. I had to keep playing till they were up. I know I've let you down, Cath. This'll be it, once and for all. I'll get your money and I'll never ask you for another penny.

Cath   Your promises mean nothing to me. She trusts me. If this is such a sure thing, how come you haven't done it before?

Johnny   I have my reasons.

Cath   What?

Johnny   Never mind what. I have my reasons.

Cath   Tell me or I'm not doing it. How come the guy's beaten you the last couple of times and suddenly he's got no chance?

Johnny   Just take my word for it.

Cath   Right, I'm away.

She heads for the door.

Johnny (*stopping her*)   I've been a bit shaky lately. Under pressure. Have you heard of beta blockers?

Cath   No.

Johnny   They're pills for hypertension. They slow your heart rate and calm you down. Stop your hands shaking. When they first came out, a couple of professional snooker players started taking them, guys who'd been struggling, and suddenly they were winning tournaments again. So they were banned. The drugs, not the players. Dad was prescribed them when Ruth died. Apparently he has a heart. I took two last night and hit an eighty-five break with the black out of commission. Then I cleared the colours off their spots four times in a row without rattling a ball. I haven't played like that for three years. I could beat Frankie Fisher with both arms tied behind my back.

Johnny *and* **Patrick** *look to* **Cath**.

Cath (*to* **Patrick**)   What?

Patrick   Get four hundred. If you think better of it, you don't have to give it to him, just put it back on Monday.

Cath   And what about the holiday?

Patrick   You'll just have to come clean to Auntie Jean.

Cath   No way. I'm not getting my name dragged into the mud because of him. *Aaaarrrggghhh*. I can't believe I'm even fucking talking about it. I need to pay for the holiday tomorrow morning, so we'd need seven hundred and twenty.

Patrick   Bloody hell.

Johnny   You'll get it back tomorrow night.

Cath   Seven hundred and twenty quid!

Johnny   You did it for Rosemary.

Cath   I knew I could trust her.

Johnny   Give me a chance. It'll all be over by tomorrow night. We can take the cash straight to the shop, if you want. Pat and me will guard you.

Cath   No! Fuck! (*To* **Patrick**.) I don't know.

Patrick   Give him a chance.

Cath   If I do it and you fuck it up again I'll kill you with my bare hands.

She leaves.

Silence.

Patrick   Are they safe?

Johnny   Millions of people take them.

Patrick   Aye, prescribed by a doctor.

Johnny   Indubitably.

Patrick   God, you sound like him.

Johnny   Maybe it's the drugs. Mum and Cath are on the same antidepressants so there's a certain symmetry, as they say.

Patrick   Are they?

Johnny   You don't know everything.

Patrick   I've never claimed to. It's pretty wearing . . .

Silence.

Johnny   Golfers take them, as well.

Patrick   You're sure your guy will take the bet?

Johnny   He's always on at me for a showdown and four hundred quid is small change to him. He'll be at the club tonight. His daddy made a fortune knocking down Ravenscraig and his darling boy gets anything he wants. One of those guys that's never wanted for anything but still manages to be a mean-spirited little cunt of the first order. Nothing would give me greater pleasure than wiping the floor with him.

Patrick   Are you going to do anything about your shakiness?

Johnny   What's to be done? I just need a bit of time to sort myself out. Once this thing's off my back . . .

Patrick   Why do you have to do it yourself?

Johnny   Please tell me you're not going to mention Jesus.

Patrick   I wasn't. Why don't you go to the doctor?

Johnny   Because she'll just tell me to stop drinking and smoking. And start eating leaves.

Patrick   So?

Johnny   I can't think of anything worse. I'm not kidding. I had enough of those people at college – running, salad for lunch, drinking fucking water in the bar. Like it was imperative that they live to a ripe old age. As if they had something indispensable to offer mankind. If some book-borne virus killed off ninety-nine per cent of Humanities students, only their parents would notice. You really might as well enjoy yourself.

Patrick   Are you enjoying yourself?

Johnny   No, right now my baby brother is nipping my head, but I have been known to have a good time. I like drinking and smoking and having a laugh with like-minded people more than anything else I've come across. If I believed in *the life to come* I might feel differently, but I know that's all shite, so don't start.

Patrick   I wasn't going to.

Johnny   And it's nothing to do with Ruth. Children die constantly, as you said yourself, without rhyme or reason. I'm not that . . . self-absorbed. The other day, did you read this, a thirteen-year-old girl in America was tied up, raped, strangled and left for dead in a field. She managed to gnaw halfway through the ropes before she died of hypothermia with tears frozen in her eyes. Isn't that perfect? God must have been busy elsewhere. I think Ruth got off relatively lightly. And I'm not too bothered about attaining my own threescore years and dementia. So save your sermons for the pulpit.

Patrick   Could you give it a rest with the priest stuff? You got yourself into this mess; don't take it out on me. You still owe me fifty-eight quid from last year.

Johnny   I hadn't forgotten.

Patrick   I could do with it, as it happens.

Johnny   Jesus, Pat, give me a break.

Patrick   I gave you a break. I lent you the money. I'm only asking for it back. You'll have eighty left over when you pay Cath back.

Johnny   That's already spoken for. You'll get your money, don't worry. You'll be all right. We can't all rely on donations.

Patrick   What the hell is it you think you do? You owe me, you owe Mum, you owe Rosemary, you owe Auntie Jean, you just tried to get more off me.

Johnny   Which I know you've got.

Patrick   No, you don't.

Johnny   Yes, I do. Cath might believe you gave it all to the starving babies in Africa, but I know you better.

Patrick   Listen, don't judge everyone else by your own standards.

Johnny   OK. Swear on the Bible you haven't got it.

Patrick   I will not.

Johnny   On Ruth's grave, then.

Patrick   Away you go. That's . . . repulsive.

Johnny   OK. Just promise me, man to man.

Patrick   No! I don't need to promise or swear anything. You
can believe what you like.

Johnny   I knew it.

Patrick   You know nothing.

He starts to tidy his bedding away.

Anyway, say I did have it . . .

Johnny   That is what I just said.

Patrick   Oh, you're sharp. Say I'd just handed over the cash
when you asked me. You'd never have mentioned Frankie
Fisher. And I'd never have seen my money again. You only
suggested it when you realised I wasn't going dig you out of
trouble.

Johnny   So?

Patrick   So solving your own problems is a last resort for
you? When all else fails, you'll clean up your own mess. And
have a go at me for not doing it for you. As if I'm the problem.

Johnny   No. All I'm saying is: if you don't want to lend me
the money, have the guts to say so. I can take it. I'm a big boy.

Patrick   I've got the guts. If I had the money, I wouldn't
lend you it. You'll never sort yourself out if your first reaction
to trouble is: who's going to fix this for me?

Johnny   Are you sorting me out, now? Performing another
selfless act? Not content with feeding the poor, you're helping
your big brother see the error of his ways. Getting him to show
some gumption.

Mum *enters.*

Mum   Why aren't you at work?

Johnny   I don't start till eleven.

Mum   What about putting in some overtime and paying me back the money you owe me?

Johnny   It's a snooker club, Mum, it doesn't open till eleven.

Mum   A bloody snooker club. Thank God one of you has the nous to get their head down and make something of themselves.

Johnny   You want me to be a priest as well?

Mum   That really is a joke.

Johnny   So, what would you like me to be?

Silence.

Mum (*to* **Patrick**)   What have you got on?

Patrick   Running shorts.

Mum   What for?

Patrick   I've just been for a run.

Mum   In those? My God. You'll get arrested.

Johnny   What would you like me to be?

Mum   You know very well what I'd like you to be.

Johnny   What?

Mum   Someone who uses their God-given talents.

Johnny   But snooker doesn't count?

Mum   No, it certainly does not.

Johnny   Even if I was making a good living?

Mum   Even if you were Steve Davis. A boy with your brains. A boy who had the chance to really make something of himself.

Johnny   So what would you like me to be?

Mum   Anything!

Johnny   Anything but what I am?

Mum   Anything but a lazy, drunken scrounger like your father.

Johnny   When he was my age he was in a travesty of a marriage with two kids. I think I've done pretty well.

Mum   You know where the door is. When you're capable of paying the rent on your own place you can talk to me like that. He got his own flat in Hamilton when he was at Comet. He and Rosemary were supposed to be getting married, but he forgot to pay the rent. Did you think the landlord wouldn't notice? Twenty-two years old and he still thinks he can bury his head in the sand. And then he loses his job, in mysterious circumstances. No wonder she got shot of you. You've thrown away every chance that ever came your way. If you won the lottery you'd lose the bloody ticket.

Johnny   It's funny how Rosemary's this paragon now. You didn't have much time for her when we were going out.

Mum *goes into the kitchen.*

Johnny (*calling after her*)   You're not the only one that's had a bad year, you know.

Dad *enters in his vest and pants, looking very rough. He makes for the kitchen but sees* **Mum** *is in there. He finds his bottle of 'Irn-Bru' and sees how little is left.*

Dad (*to* **Johnny**, *quietly*)   You been at this?

Johnny   No!

Dad *places the bottle out of sight, then picks it up, takes a sip and puts it back.*

Dad (*to* **Patrick**)   What have you come as?

Mum *comes in from the kitchen.*

Mum   So what's for breakfast?

Dad   You talking to me?

Mum   Who else would I be talking to?

Dad   I haven't the foggiest notion.

Mum   Who else is in charge of the fiscal planning?

Dad   What are you talking about?

Mum   Where's the salad? The steak? The forty pairs of shoes?

Dad   Are you all right? Have you gone insane overnight?

Mum   You told us last night that you had plenty of money and you'd be supplying all our dietary and footwear requirements.

Dad   Give me peace.

Mum   Didn't he, Patrick?

Patrick *would rather not get involved.*

Mum   Didn't he?

Patrick   Do you want me to run up to the shops?

Johnny   I thought you had no money.

Patrick   I haven't. I mean I don't mind going if somebody stumps up.

Mum   Your father holds the purse strings now.

Patrick   Have you got any money, Dad?

Dad   Oh, I've got money all right. Don't you worry about that.

Patrick   Can I have some?

Dad   What for?

Patrick   So I can go and get breakfast?

Dad   Food is your mother's department.

Mum   Not as of last night. You heard him, Johnny, didn't you? 'I'm in charge of the fiscal planning. I'll make sure these kids are properly fed. This second.'

Johnny *says nothing.*

Mum   Am I going mad? Did he or didn't he?

Johnny   Going to leave me out of it?

Mum   I'm asking for a simple statement of fact. Did he or did he not say that? Patrick?

Patrick   I just want some breakfast. I'm happy to run up to McCormick's and get some rolls, if somebody supplies me with the wherewithal.

Dad   Looks like you've finally cracked. All your pill-popping has finally caught up with you. Funny how someone who says they believe in eternal life in paradise needs pills to get through the day. I'd have thought you'd need something to stop you singing and dancing.

Mum   Don't you dare make fun of my faith.

Dad   I wouldn't dream of it. I'm making fun of your drug addiction.

Patrick   You did say those things.

Dad   Eh?

Patrick   You did say those things.

Dad   I said what?

Patrick   What she said.

Dad   Oh I did, did I? I said what she said, did I?

Patrick   Yeah.

Dad   Is that right?

Patrick   Yeah.

Dad   Is that right? Well, there you are.

Silence.

Mum   I'm going to Mass. You coming?

Patrick   No.

Mum   It's the first Friday of the month.

Patrick   I've been to Mass every day for five years, Mum. I've got other things to do.

Mum   Like what?

Patrick   Just stuff.

Mum   What stuff?

Patrick   Personal stuff.

Mum   What kind of personal stuff?

Patrick   The personal kind you don't tell your mum about.

Mum   Oh, God, don't tell me.

Patrick   What?

Mum   Not you as well?

Patrick   What are you on about?

Mum   Have they kicked you out?

Patrick   Who?

Mum   You know damn well who. The priests.

Patrick   Don't be daft. Why would they kick me out?

Mum   I don't know. What have you done?

Patrick   Nothing! It's got nothing to do with the priests. Or the seminary. Or you, for that matter. You'll be late for Mass.

Mum   Promise me there's nothing wrong.

Patrick   No.

Mum   What do you mean, 'No'?

Patrick   No. Go.

Mum   I knew it.

Patrick   What?

Mum   I knew something was up.

Patrick   Nothing's up.

Mum   This family will be the death of me.

She leaves.

Silence.

Dad (*to* **Patrick**)   I'm just going to get dressed. I want to talk to you.

Patrick   OK.

Dad   Don't move.

Patrick   I won't.

Dad (*to* **Johnny**)   Alone.

He exits.

Johnny   Watch yourself.

Patrick   What? I just told the truth. I'm not scared of him.

Johnny   Well, you should be.

Patrick   Well, I'm not. I can look after myself.

Johnny   You think?

Patrick   I know. I'm not twelve years old any more, in case you hadn't noticed.

Johnny   It doesn't matter how old you are.

Patrick   How do you make that out?

Johnny   Did you do a lot of fighting in the seminary?

Patrick   Some.

Johnny   It won't have prepared you for him.

Patrick   Don't worry about me. I can handle him.

Johnny (*laughing*)   Listen to the big man.

Patrick *starts to put on yesterday's clothes.*

Patrick   Laugh away. At least I had the nerve to stand up to him.

Johnny   I've stood up to him plenty. What do you know? You've been tucked away in your private school for five years.

Patrick   It's not a private school.

Johnny   Mum pays fees, doesn't she?

Patrick   It's five pounds a week, if you can afford it. Nothing, if you can't.

Johnny   But she pays it, doesn't she? Even though she can't afford it.

Patrick   I don't know.

Johnny   There's quite a lot you don't know. Remember I got beaten up by those guys from Garrion Academy? You'd have been thirteen. They broke one of my ribs and it punctured my lung?

Patrick   Course. You did that trick in the hospital. Making the big jar of water bubble when you coughed.

Johnny   I'd forgotten that. Remember what Dad said he was going to do to the guys that did it?

Patrick   Did he get them?

Johnny   They didn't exist. As he well knew.

Silence.

Patrick   You have got to be joking.

Johnny *(getting his stuff together)*   I wish I was. He'd been having a go at Mum, and I cracked and told him to shut his fucking mouth. And he did. He stopped. I felt pretty fucking pleased with myself. He met me off the bus from school the next day, took me up to the Fields and punched me till I couldn't get up. Marquis of Queensberry Rules, mind, like he taught us. He panicked when he realised how bad it was and we cooked up the gang story. Three guys from the Academy on the hunt for Catholics. It was my idea. I had to walk to a phone box and call the ambulance. I thought I was having a heart attack. Don't tell him I told you.

Patrick   I won't. That's absolutely terrible.

Johnny   There's no point standing up to him. You can't change him. I'm going to get some practice in. Will you phone Cath later? Give her a nudge?

Patrick   I'll go and see her. I'm sorry, that's absolutely terrible.

Johnny *leaves.*

Patrick *goes to the sideboard and retrieves a locked diary. The key is on a chain round his neck. He unlocks the diary, then goes to the door to check that* **Dad** *isn't imminent. He holds the diary upside down and flicks through the pages. Lots of banknotes flutter to the carpet. He hurriedly gathers them up and puts them in his pockets. He sits.*

Dad *enters.*

Dad   So what was that about?

Patrick   What?

Dad   You know damn well what. Don't fuck with me, son.

Patrick   You did say you had money.

Dad   I have got money. More money than you could imagine.

Patrick   What's the problem, then?

Dad   Whose house is this?

Patrick   What's that got to do with it?

Dad   Whose house is it?

Patrick   It's a council flat and you and Mum are the tenants.

Dad   It's mine and mine alone.

Patrick   It's as much Mum's as it is yours.

Dad Oh, is that right? Says who? You? I'm the boss in this house, son, and the sooner you learn that the easier it'll be for you. You know where the door is. If you want to stay, you abide by my rules.

Patrick What are they?

Dad Don't make me lose my temper. So help me God. You're not too old to be taught a lesson.

Patrick I don't know what it is you want from me.

Dad I want a bit of respect. I want you to accept that I am the boss in this house.

Patrick I accept that you and Mum are the bosses.

Dad Me and me alone.

Patrick No.

Dad No? What do you mean, 'No'?

Patrick I don't accept that you and you alone are in charge.

Dad Let's clear a bit of space.

Patrick What for?

Dad To see who's boss.

He moves a chair back against the window. He moves the couch against the door. He pushes the other chair against the wall.

Come on then, son.

He adopts a convincing-looking boxing stance.

Come on, son, what's stopping you? Let's see what you can do.

Patrick Not in here.

Dad Here'll do fine.

Patrick Not enough room. Supposed to be twenty-four by twenty-four, isn't it?

Dad I'm glad you remember something I taught you. Now I'm going to teach you something else. Come on.

Patrick Let's go up the Fields.

Dad   You looking for someone to break it up?

Patrick   There's hardly ever a soul up there. It's the perfect place for a fight, the Fields, is it not?

Dad (*unsettled*)   Come on, let's get it done.

Patrick   Let's go up the Fields. That'd be an ideal venue, I'd say.

Dad   What have the fucking Fields got to do with anything? Never mind the fucking Fields.

Patrick   I'll take you on up the Fields. Come on.

He shifts the couch and opens the door.

If you're not up there in ten minutes, I'll assume you've had a change of heart.

He leaves.

Dad *goes for his poteen.*

Lights.

3   Friday Night

The couch is still blocking the door. **Dad** *is lying on it, out for the count. Two empty Irn Bru bottles lie nearby.* **Mum** *sits in one chair reading the* Daily Record, **Cath** *sits in the other with a can of 'Coke'.*

Patrick *squeezes through the door.*

Patrick   What's happened here?

Mum   When were you going to tell me?

Patrick   What?

Mum   I had to hear it from Tommy McGuire.

Patrick   What?

Mum   That you've left the seminary. Tommy's sister's boy phoned home last night and told her you'd just said goodbye and walked out. Tommy came up to me after Mass to commiserate. It was all he could do to keep from smirking. I knew the holiday's weren't till next week.

Patrick   I was going to tell you tomorrow.

Mum   Why?

Patrick   It's a long story, Mum. I'm not cut out to be a priest.

Mum   How do you know?

Patrick   Believe me, I know.

Mum   Why didn't you tell me straight away? Why did I have to hear it from Tommy?

Patrick   Sorry about that.

Mum   Oh, don't worry, I didn't let on that I didn't know. I wouldn't give him the satisfaction. What are you going to do?

Patrick   I'm not sure.

Mum   But you'll be going to university?

Patrick *perches on an arm of the couch.*

Patrick   I need to think about it. There's no rush; it's too late to get into uni this year.

Mum   Why?

Patrick   I didn't apply.

Mum   Why not?

Patrick   I didn't know this was going to happen.

Mum   Surely they'd make an exception. In the circumstances.

Patrick   I don't want them to. They'll take me next year.

Mum   You'll be a year behind.

Patrick   I don't care about that.

Mum   I do.

Patrick   Mum, with all respect, it's not your problem. If I think it's the most useful thing I can do, I'll go next year.

Mum   What do you mean, 'if'?

Patrick   You know what 'if' means.

Mum   Oh God, not another one. Please, not another one. Please tell me you're not thinking of not going to university.

Patrick   I'm certainly not going to go because you want me to. Or to demonstrate how clever I am. It needs to be for the right reasons.

Mum   Five years down the drain just like that?

Patrick   Nothing's down the drain.

Mum (*pointing at* **Dad**)   Look! Are you blind? Johnny won all the prizes at St Ignatius before you did and now he serves lager in a snooker hall for a living.

Patrick   Listen to me: I'm going to do something with my life.

Mum   That's what I thought. Everybody thinks that.

Patrick   Well, I am. Or I'll die trying.

Mum   What (*are you going to do*)?

Patrick   Something that . . .

Mum   You see? You have no idea. It's a fantasy.

Patrick   I want the world to be better rather than worse for my having existed.

Mum   God Almighty. I can't believe my ears.

Cath   What's wrong with that?

Mum   Don't you encourage him. Did something happen to you in the seminary?

Patrick   What like?

Mum   You know.

Patrick   What?

Mum   I saw a thing in the paper. A priest . . . took advantage of a boy.

Patrick   No!

Mum   What, then? If you want to make the world a better place, why did you leave?

Patrick   I don't want to talk about that just now. You were dead against me going in the first place, remember.

Mum   I want to know.

Patrick   Mum, listen to me, this is important. That's my final offer. I'll tell you later or I won't tell you at all. I'm serious.

Silence.

Mum (*getting up*)   I never liked the idea of them taking twelve-year-old boys away from their families. What are all those Italian priests doing in Scotland? Are there not enough boys in Italy for them to train?

She squeezes out of the door.

Patrick *sits in* **Mum**'s *chair.*

Patrick   Did you get it?

Cath   Yup.

Patrick   Great.

Cath   That doesn't mean I'm going to give it to him.

Patrick   It's up to you. I think it'll work out. I really do.

Silence.

Cath   Have you tried talking to Ruth?

Patrick   No. Have you?

Cath   Yeah.

Patrick   And?

Cath   I don't know. Nothing I could make out. She'd have done anything for Johnny. She adored him. She was in awe of you, but she adored Johnny.

Patrick   I know. I wish I'd known her a bit better. She was only seven when I went away.

The toilet flushes.

Cath   Why don't we go to a medium? I know some of them are charlatans, but don't you think some of them might have a gift?

Patrick   I've got a better idea. I've got a proposition for you.

Mum *squeezes back through the door.* **Patrick** *gets up from* **Mum***'s chair and goes to perch on the arm of the couch again.*

Mum *sits down.*

Patrick   Can he not sleep in his bloody bed?

Mum   Rearranging the furniture must have tired him out.

Patrick   Dad, do you think I could have a seat? Dad?

Cath   You'll be lucky.

Patrick *gives him a shake.*

Patrick   Dad, can I get a seat?

He gives him another shake.

Dad! I want a seat. Wake up.

He shakes him hard.

Dad!

No response.

How long's he been there?

Mum   He was there when I came in about three.

Patrick   That's four hours, Mum. Has he moved at all?

He picks up one of the Irn-Bru bottles and sniffs it.

Cath   He's been farting like a camel.

Mum   That's enough of that, you.

Patrick (*shaking him*)   Dad! . . . Dad!

He takes his pulse.

Dad! . . . Dad!

He slaps his face.

Cath   Is he dead?

Patrick *tries to put him in recovery position.*

Patrick   No.

Mum   What a shame.

Cath   Mum!

Mum   He's alive. I can speak ill of the living, can't I?

Cath   He's your husband.

Mum   Don't remind me.

Cath   You shouldn't wish anyone dead.

Mum   Why not? The world would be a better place without him. This house would certainly be a better place without him.

Cath   Stop it! He might die. How would you feel then?

Patrick   I'll run round to Pete's and phone an ambulance.

He exits.

Cath *and* **Mum** *look down at* **Dad***. What if this was his last day on earth?*

Mum   Look at the state of him. He was the best-looking man I'd ever seen.

She puts her ear to his chest. She shakes him.

That's the first time I've laid a hand on him in years.

Dad *stands up and picks up an empty Irn-Bru bottle.*

Dad   What about this? What about this? Your Royal
Highnesses (though I have to say I think the monarchy should
be . . . *abolished* forthwith), Lords –

Cath   Dad, are you OK? Are you still asleep?

Dad   Shh, now. I've got to get this before it goes. Just be
quiet. Your Royal Highnesses, Lords (they should be abolished
as well), Ladies (they should never have been invented) and
Gentlemen (by which I mean the ordinary working man),
Members of the Committee, I'm delighted to accept the Nobel
Prize for . . .

Somebody asked me, it was Burt Lancaster . . . Cassius Clay.
It certainly beats IRA assassins hiding in your clothes. In your
wardrobe.

Mum   John, for God's sake . . .

Dad   Shh. I'll lose it. There were five of them and I grabbed
one and bit his fucking nose off. Then I battered the rest of
them while they pleaded for mercy, snivelling like wee boys.

Anyway, Michael Parkinson asked me how it felt to win the,
eh . . . Prize, the . . . big prize, the . . . big, big prize, and I just
said, 'Well, Michael . . . '

He stands on the couch.

'Listen, Parky, I'm just an ordinary man. I don't want money
or titles or special treatment. I wouldn't drink in the Stag if
you paid me a million dollars.' I had a book out, called *You'll
Never Learn Anything from a Book.*

Cath   Sit down, Dad, and I'll get you a cup of tea.

Dad   Please! For the last time! If I hadn't become a
successful . . . I could be Secretary General of the Transport
and General . . . No. No, no, no. The United Nations, and that's
the important thing: I could have been anything. Anything.
And that's what matters. Everybody knows what I have inside
me. Everybody that matters. And the people that don't know,
don't matter. Let all the blowhards and phoneys run around
in their cars, collecting awards and doing things to women.

Getting beautiful women to follow their instructions to the letter. 'Take your clothes off. Turn round. Bend over that chair.'

Mum *leaves.*

Dad   I don't care about that stuff. I know and you know and that's that. It's for other people to speculate about whether I'm the greatest man in history, it's a matter of complete indifference to me. I just want to turn my back on everything. Goodnight.

He falls over the back of the couch.

Lights.

4   Saturday Night

Cath *is alone. A bit out of it. She lights a candle and drips wax onto a saucer. She stands the candle in the saucer, then turns off the light.*

Cath (*never sentimental*)   Ruth? Ruth Conlan? Hello, if you're there. Is there anything I have to do?

If you want to contact me, I won't be afraid. Just give me a sign.

I miss you.

Are you OK? Or does that not mean anything any more?

Where are you? Are you someone else? Are the Buddhists right? Or is it the Hindus? I'm still really ignorant. Don't tell me it's the Jews. Sorry. You might be a Jew now. Sorry.

Should I be quiet?

Are you still a child?

Oh, you were the loveliest thing. It breaks my heart not to hold you and squash you any more. You were such a little stick. It makes me want to die.

I do want to die. Often. (*Amused.*) I don't mean I want to die often, just once will do. I often want to die, is what I mean.

If I thought I'd get to touch you I'd come and join you right now. If you opened a door in space, I wouldn't look back.

Will I be OK? I might be in the shit. I might lose my job on Monday. It doesn't matter. I'm in the shit whatever happens.

You've probably moved on to better things. I hope you have. You probably don't have time for us.

Maybe you're part of a bigger family. Maybe you don't even remember us.

You know Dad's in hospital? I think he'll live, unless hangovers can be terminal.

Mind you, I didn't realise you could die of an asthma attack.

There's no smoking in the house any more, we have to go outside. Even though we all smoke. Well, Pat doesn't, but even while he's away.

Pat's watching Johnny play snooker for money. Do you know about that? They should be back soon.

Don't be offended if I stop talking to you suddenly. I don't want them taking the piss out of me.

They wouldn't take the piss. They'd think I was a bit sad. Which I can do without.

I'm sorry our family was so hopeless.

We're hopeless.

Apparently, Pat has a plan.

Please speak to me if you can. I've got one more thing to say, then I'll shut up.

Forgive us for carrying on without you – there was nothing else to do.

Long silence.

Cath *suddenly looks at the sideboard.*

She switches on the light, goes to the sideboard and opens the half that **Johnny** *baulked at on Thursday night. It's crammed with Ruth's things. School uniform, clothes, toys, book bag, photos, inhalers. She begins to empty it.*

She removes a slip of paper from the book bag and holds it up.

They cancelled that trip because of you. You didn't even miss it.

Patrick *enters.*

Cath   How'd it go?

Patrick   No.

Cath   Oh Jesus. That's that then.

Patrick   He was four–one up. He only needed one frame and he fell apart. One frame.

Silence.

Cath   At least Auntie Jean's got her holiday. It'll be *me* that gets the jail.

Patrick   What if you come clean to Mrs Calder? Explain how Johnny put you in an impossible position, that the two of you will pay it back.

Cath (*scratching her neck*)   She'd be on the phone to the police before I'd finished a sentence.

Patrick   Will you stop scratching?

Cath   I'll do what I damn well like.

Patrick   You're just making it worse.

Cath   I know! I don't care! That's how bad it is. You have no idea.

Patrick   You should never have done it, you know.

Cath   You told me to do it.

Patrick   No, you shouldn't have given him Auntie Jean's money. He stole from his work, he should have taken his medicine. It might have done him some good.

Cath   Johnny would be lost in jail.

Patrick   He wouldn't have gone to jail, with Ruth and everything. Neither will you. You shouldn't have done it.

Cath   Aye, so you said. But I did do it. And I will take the consequences, OK?

Patrick   You don't need to take the consequences.

Cath   How do you work that out?

Patrick   Because I'll have to take the effing consequences.

Cath   How?

Patrick   I've got the money.

Silence.

Cath   Does Johnny know?

Patrick   I told him when it got to four–three. It didn't help, obviously.

Cath   What did he say?

Patrick   That he didn't need it. Big talk. As usual.

Cath   Where is he?

Patrick   Don't know. He stormed off. I think he went to the Stag with wee Higgy. He knows he's in the clear.

He takes the money from his pockets and counts out £720. He has a couple of hundred left.

Here.

Cath   I don't want it.

Patrick   Don't be daft.

Cath   It's yours. I'll take my medicine.

Patrick   Take it. I told you to get the money.

Cath   I've got a mind of my own.

Patrick   I want you to take it. I don't want you to get into trouble.

Cath   Aye, but like you said, it's my own fault. I'm resigned to my fate. I really believed you didn't have it.

Patrick   I was going to tell you earlier but something came up.

Cath   What?

Patrick   I had to do something at short notice.

Cath   Sure you weren't letting me suffer for my sins?

Patrick   Positive. Take it. I'd have given you it in the end, anyway, if he hadn't suggested the bet. I just didn't like the way he was talking to me.

Cath   And you wanted him to sweat for it.

Patrick   I didn't see why he shouldn't sweat for it. And I thought he'd pull it off.

Cath   Do you think he's OK?

Patrick   Well, he won't like being deposed, but he knows he's off the hook. He was great and then he was terrible. I don't think he believed he could win, when it came to it. He wasn't the only one that was sweating. Look at it that way. I lost my gamble and now I'm paying up.

Cath   But that was only for four hundred.

Patrick   For God's sake, Cath, just take it. It's priest money anyway; I'm not entitled any more.

He pushes it into her hand.

(*Irish accent.*) That's for you. Don't tell your mother.

Cath *doesn't hand it back.*

Cath   I'll pay you back. Thanks. Do you want a drink?

Patrick   What is there?

Cath   Just vodka and Coke, I'm afraid.

Patrick   I've been drinking lager.

Cath   Vodka's fine with anything. It's pure.

Patrick   OK. Thanks.

Cath *goes to the kitchen.*

Patrick What are you doing? Is this Ruth's stuff?

Cath *(off)* I was trying to talk to her. I was talking to her. I was trying to get her to talk back.

Patrick Any luck?

Cath *(off)* I don't know. How do you know?

Silence. **Patrick** *looks through Ruth's things.*

Cath *(off)* Why did you leave the seminary?

Patrick I had to.

Cath *(off)* They didn't kick you out?

Patrick No, they wanted me to stay. *I* wanted to stay.

Cath *(off)* So why didn't you?

Patrick I wasn't really eligible.

Cath *(off)* How not?

Patrick *doesn't reply.*

Cath *enters with two glasses, gives one to* **Patrick**.

Patrick Ta.

Cath Cheers.

They clink glasses.

Patrick Cheers.

They drink.

Long silence.

Cath Are you gay?

Patrick No!

Cath It wouldn't bother me if you were.

Patrick It would bother me.

Silence.

I don't believe the Bible. I don't believe Jesus was the son of God. Or his mother was a virgin. Or that God rescued the Jews from Pharaoh's army but had given up miracles by the time Hitler's arrived. I don't think there is a God.

Cath Because of Ruth?

Patrick I don't think I ever believed.

Cath You must have done.

Patrick I used to *know* He existed, like I knew Santa Claus existed. I thought it was a fact because people I trusted told me it was. The funny thing is, the more you study the scriptures – who wrote them, when they were written, why they were written, who they were written for – the more you realise they're just propaganda. When you start thinking for yourself, it all falls apart. Not that I was ever all that religious.

Cath That's what Mum says. Why the hell did you go in the first place?

Patrick They didn't talk about God much when they came round the schools. It was all about building hospitals and schools, digging ditches. And they weren't like parish priests, you know? Wee mean Irishmen trying to frighten the life out of you. They were big lively Italians with black beards going 'Do you want to make the world a better place?'

Cath I remember. They came to my class, too.

Patrick And they are good men. It's a good life, you know, a proper community. Eating together, studying together, playing football, singing. It was the perfect place for a boy who needed to leave home. I went from here with the telly on all day every day, to watching it about twice a year, when Scotland had a big game.

Cath I would hate that.

Patrick You think so, but I bet you wouldn't. Every day before dinner they have 'Time of the Spirit'. No one is allowed to speak for twenty minutes. You all wander through the grounds in total silence. You can think about God or girls or playing for Celtic and no one can disturb you.

Cath   I like the sound of that. They should make that the Law of the Land.

Patrick   It was the best thing I ever did.

Cath   Can't you stick it out? You might change your mind.

Patrick   I have stuck it out. The last two years I've been hanging on. I was in the sickroom one night after an asthma attack, listening to the boys playing football outside, feeling sorry for myself, and Father Borghese came up and carried me down to the side of the pitch in a blanket. I wasn't a favourite of his but I knew he wasn't doing it for me, it was because of his love for Jesus. And in the end you have to do everything out of love for Jesus, or it's just philanthropy, and philanthropy isn't good enough, apparently. You have to believe in the Resurrection, and I don't. For Jesus or Ruth or anyone else.

Silence.

I've got an appointment to see a housing officer on Monday.

Cath   You're not leaving us as well, are you?

Patrick   I'm leaving here.

Cath   Already?

Patrick   I had a run-in with Dad yesterday.

Cath   Never mind him.

Patrick   I do mind him. And so should you. And not just him. This is not a proper way to live. It's poisonous.

Cath   It's not that bad.

Patrick   You think things are OK here?

Cath   I don't know about OK. Normal.

Patrick   That's the worst thing. To think it's normal.

Cath   It is normal.

Patrick   Is it normal for a girl with her whole life ahead of her to be on antidepressants?

Cath (*beginning to bristle*)   It is, actually. I know lots.

Patrick   You've every right to be depressed.

Cath   I am fucking depressed.

Patrick   But what are you doing about it?

Cath   I'm taking antidepressants, you cretin.

Patrick   Have you heard of Liberation Theology?

She looks at him.

Cath   Aye, it's all we ever talk about in the Stag.

Patrick   There are Catholics who think that the Church actually helps to keep oppressed people down – to put up with injustice in this life because it will all be sorted out in the next. In fact, the more you suffer, the better. But Jesus said, 'I come not to bring peace, but a sword.' Anyway. Heaven and alcohol and pills are all ways of coping with things as they are, instead of changing them.

Cath   What the fuck do you know about it? You've just swanned in here after five years of people being nice and holy to each other. The real world is a very hard place, Patrick Conlan. You wait. Where do you think the council will move you to?

Patrick   I don't know.

Cath   I do. Stonebridge. Any money. Then you'll see what it's all about. There are plenty of empty flats in Stonebridge. The McCluskeys down the stairs, with their two-bedroom flat like this, they turned down a semi-detached house with a garden in Stonebridge. The *McCluskeys*, with five kids and three dogs and barely a full set of teeth between them.

Patrick   It'll be better than living here. You won't get better here. Nobody could get better here. Your skin won't get better, you won't come off the pills, you won't lose weight.

Cath   What's my weight got to do with it?

Patrick   You happy with it?

Cath   What's that got to do with you?

Patrick   Nothing, if you're happy with it . . .

Silence.

I'm going to ask for a two-bedroom flat.

Silence.

Will you consider it?

Silence.

I've got a little bit of money left. Not as much as I'd hoped, obviously. I'll get a job while a ponder my next move. What do you think?

Cath *is thinking.*

Cath   What if your next move is away? You're not going to want to stay in Stonebridge for long. You'll be off to uni and I'll be on my own in the Buckfast Triangle.

Patrick   It's a ten-minute walk to Motherwell station. The train to Glasgow takes fifteen minutes. I could go to uni no bother.

Cath   Aye, but will you?

Patrick   I don't know.

Silence.

Cath   And what about Mum?

Patrick   I was nine when I first asked her to take us away.

Cath   I've asked her myself.

Patrick   Not because it's all his fault but because they –

Cath   It is all his fault.

Patrick   They're awful together. They belong apart. But she'll never give in. You're in the middle of the Thirty Years

War here. I wouldn't drag all that shit into my new life even if I could.

Cath   What about Johnny?

Patrick   He needs to sort himself out. I'm not looking for a dependant.

Cath   Ruth broke his heart. Then Rosemary dumped him. Mind you, he slept with her best friend.

Patrick   Did he?

Cath   He owes her money as well.

Patrick   He probably owed Ruth money.

Cath *laughs.*

Cath   Maybe he bumped her off.

Patrick   He might have had the motive, but would he have the initiative?

Cath   That's terrible.

Patrick   What do you think?

Cath *thinks.*

Patrick   We'll eat better. Pasta, vegetables. Instead of chips every bloody night.

Cath   I love chips. Dad says that when I was little I went to the chippy and asked if they had anything greasy for 10p.

Patrick   That's one of his standard jokes about fat people, Cath.

Cath   Thanks very much.

Patrick   I bet you'd notice a big difference in your skin. Do you not think if you were a bit fitter and your skin was better you might not need pills?

Cath   That's one of the things I miss about Ruth. She thought I was great. She didn't realise I was a fat scaly wreck.

Silence.

Patrick   I think you're great.

Silence.

We could have our own 'Time of the Spirit'.

Cath   It's a nice idea.

Patrick   What's to stop us? We can live any life we choose. We can do anything.

Cath   I'll think about it.

She starts to put Ruth's things away.

I'm thinking about it.

Lights.

5   Sunday Night

A fortnight later, post-autopsy. There's an open coffin in the sitting room.

We hear the toilet flush, then **Dad** *enters, dressed in a suit, shirt and tie. He sits and pours himself another whisky.*

After a while he gets up and looks into the coffin.

He sits back down.

He gets up and looks in the coffin again.

Dad   You're better off out of it. I hope to God I join you shortly.

He goes back to his seat and drinks.

He gets back up and looks in the coffin.

He sits.

He gets back up and goes to the coffin.

He reaches in and touches the body.

Where have you gone?

He looks up.

Can you hear me?

He waits.

If there's a God, let me know.

He waits.

Make that picture fall off the wall and I'll clean up my act.

He looks at the picture for some time.

He sits back down.

Heaven would be fucking hellish, anyway. Full of phoneys and holy Joes. And women. (*To the ceiling*) You can keep it. You can shove your fucking paradise up your arse. And your angels and your saints. I'd rather burn in Hell than spend eternity with all those miserable cunts singing your praises. 'I believe in one God, the Father, the Almighty, the maker of Heaven and Earth, of Motherwell and Wishaw, of Morecambe and Wise . . . You provide for the birds of the field, who neither reap nor sow; you lay me down in pastures; you take away the sins of the world; you smite my enemies; your house has many mansions.' What does that mean? 'Peter, do you love me, feed my sheep; if anyone comes to Me, and does not hate his own father and mother and wife and children, yes, and even his own life, he cannot be My disciple.' We might have some common ground after all, Your Warship. 'Yay and I say unto you that unless a rich man surrender all that he owns and takes a sword to his family then his camel cannot enter the assbone of a giraffe.'

He refills his glass and raises it to God.

'For now we see through a glass, darkly, but then we shall see face to face.' Send me to Hell, by all means, if that's what you want. No doubt I belong there. I couldn't care less. How about that, big man? You have no power over me. Do you feel a wee bit inadequate? If you send me to burn in Hell I will turn the other cheek. I refuse to bow to your tyranny. You and all the rest.

Mum *enters. She goes to the coffin and crosses herself.*

Mum   Hail, Mary, full of grace, the Lord is with thee. Blessed art thou amongst women and blessed is the fruit of thy womb, Jesus. Holy Mary, mother of God, pray for us sinners now and at the hour of our death, Amen.

She gets a Wishaw Press *and a* Hamilton Advertiser *from her bag. She sits and reads.*

The toilet flushes then **Cath** *enters. She sits by* **Mum***.*

Mum *hands* **Cath** *a paper. They read.*

Silence.

Mum   I quite like this one.

Cath   I like the display, it's a bit big, though, don't you think?

Mum   Maybe a bit.

They read.

Cath   God Almighty. Listen to this:

> 'We know you had to go,
> But still we miss you so.
> We wish that God could tell us why
> He had to take such a lovely guy,
> And that you had to die.
>
> If you could have spoken before you died,
> These are the words you would have sighed:
> Do not shed a tear for me,
> God has come to set me free.
>
> The gates of Heaven opened wide,
> The angels lined up side by side,
> A very special man walked inside.
>
> We love you and we always will,
> Your place no one could ever fill.
> We never will forget you, Bill.'

She looks to **Mum***.*

Mum   What's wrong with that?

Cath   Why do they have to rhyme?

Mum   I think it's lovely.

Cath   Why can't we just say what we feel?

No reply.

I'm not doing a rhyme.

Dad *gets up and fetches a bookie's pen and a one-armed pair of specs from his jacket, then a torn utility-bill envelope from the windowsill. He sits back down and starts composing.*

Cath
   'My heart aches since you fell asleep
   Your memories I'll always keep
   From tears and sorrow we know you're free
   And in our hearts you'll always be.'

Fell asleep. I hate that.

Dad
   So my poem will nearly rhyme
   Back to front I'll put this line.

Patrick *enters. He looks rough.*

Patrick   Hiya.

Cath   Hiya.

Dad   Whoof! You look like you had a good night.

Patrick   Oh aye. Terrific.

He goes to look at **Johnny***'s body. He wants to pray, but to whom? He looks at his watch.*

Patrick   When are we supposed to be there?

Cath   They can't take Johnny up till evening Mass is out. So, say it finishes at quarter to, give Father Trench time to get out of his vestments . . . ten past seven?

Dad   I saw him in the Cross Keys last night, he was completely out of his vestments.

Cath   He doesn't drink.

Dad Aye, so he tells his flock.

Cath He'd have to be pretty stupid to –

Mum Don't rise to the bait. Don't give him the satisfaction.

Dad How's the mission to Stonebridge? Have you made any converts? Or are you just teaching them to use cutlery at this stage in the operation?

Mum Haven't you heard your son's become an atheist?

Dad I'm glad to hear it.

Patrick (*to* **Mum**) It's not a choice. I can't help it. I just don't believe.

Mum So all the priests have got it wrong? The Pope, Mother Teresa, Padre Pio, Cardinal Newman, all the saints, all the Catholics in the world have got it wrong, and you're right?

Patrick It's no different from thinking all the Protestants and Jews and Muslims are wrong.

Mum They are wrong.

Dad Marx was bang on, son – 'Religion is the opiate of the people.'

Mum If only it was. Alcohol is the opiate of the people.

Dad And here's to it . . .

He drinks some whisky.

At least alcohol exists.

He drinks again.

(*To* **Mum**.) You can wait for your reward in the next life, I'll take mine the now, just in case.

Mum (*to* **Patrick**) So you're born, you die and that's it?

Patrick You're born, you live, you die.

Mum And Johnny's just gone now, is he? It was all for nothing?

Patrick How do I know, Mum?

Mum   Have you been drinking?

Patrick   I've had a couple.

Mum   Here we go. It always starts with a couple.

Patrick   Nothing's starting. It's been a hard week. I'm not a drinker.

Mum   Neither was he, neither was Johnny.

Patrick   That's got nothing to do with me. Leave me alone.

Mum   *I* had a crisis after Ruth died. I didn't understand how God could let that happen to me. I was in this very room at my wits' end when I heard buzzing and there was a wasp trying to get out of that window. You know how I can't stand wasps. So I opened the window as wide as I could but it just kept bumping up and down the glass. So I got a cushion and tried to get the wasp onto it so I could poke it out the window and let it fly off, but it didn't like that and it started to get angry, and I start talking to it, 'I'm only trying to help you, you stupid thing.' But how could it understand? It didn't even know what a cushion was or that a solid object can be transparent. How could it comprehend me, whose brain is hundreds of times the size of its whole body? How do you know you're not bumping against the glass?

Patrick   I don't.

Mum   (*pointing at* **Dad**)   Is that how you want to end up? Take a good look. Go on. Because that's what happens when you don't believe in anything bigger than yourself. You don't know how to endure. That's why he has to knock himself out every night. If he had to put his head on the pillow sober, he'd never sleep again.

Dad   I don't know how to endure? That's a good one. That's a cracker. I don't know how to endure. Sure, what else have I been doing for the last twenty-five years? Getting up in the dark in all weathers and knocking my pan out. Coming home to you every night with your face tripping you. I don't know how to endure? All I know is how to endure.

Patrick   Have you written anything down?

Cath   Not really. We've tried. We're struggling.

Patrick   I know. I haven't either.

Dad   I don't see why we have to write his sermon for him.

Patrick   We don't. Just if there's anything we particularly want said. Like we did for Ruth. Are you doing it now?

Dad   No, I'm composing verse for the paper. How about this?

'I wish my pills
Had cured your ills
And I was dead
Instead.'

Mum   Do you think it's funny?

Dad   What's funny about that? I mean it.

Cath   Don't argue. Please. Should I say about his fan club?

Mum   What about it?

Cath   Just that he had one. I was really nervous starting high school and it made me feel, you know, sort of special that fourth-year girls had badges with his picture.

Mum   Where did it get him? Star footballer and class clown.

Cath   It's just a nice memory.

Patrick   Do you want me to write it down?

Cath   Is it silly?

Patrick   No. It's what you remember.

He writes it down.

What about you, Mum?

Mum   What is there to say? I don't agree with all this parading your emotions.

Silence.

Cath (*to* **Patrick**)   You must have something.

Patrick   I just keep wondering how he went from top of the class at eleven to stealing from Comet at twenty-one.

Mum   There'll be no mention of stealing. Or of Comet for that matter. Are you mad?

Patrick   I wasn't going to mention stealing. But how did he end up working there?

Dad   Why shouldn't he steal from Comet? What do Comet do but steal?

Mum   There's your answer. Right there.

Cath   Mum, don't.

Dad   Plenty of people steal and live to a hundred. They give knighthoods for stealing.

Mum   I begged him. I actually got down on my knees, Cath'll back me up, I got down on my knees and begged him to go to college and retake his Highers.

Cath   It's true.

Mum   And when he blew his grant on clothes and booze, I paid his fares out of my own pocket and bought his books while his father sat in the pub. I warned him repeatedly. 'Get your exams and take yourself off to university or you'll end up in a job that you hate and you won't be able to stick it out. I know you. You'll regret it for the rest of your life.'

Dad   I fail to see how he wasn't encouraged by that pep talk.

Mum   And now your other son wants to throw his life away and you just sit there. Again.

Dad   What do you want me to do? If he's as intelligent as you think he is, he can make his mind up for himself.

Mum   That's it, is it? That's the sum total of your advice for your only surviving son?

Dad   I went to the only university that counts: the university of life.

Mum   I wish to God you'd dropped out.

Dad   Very good. (*To* **Patrick**.) I'd been twice round the world by the time I was your age. I'd seen sharks in the Panama Canal. I saw Paul Robeson at Carnegie Hall. Don't ask me why I came back here.

Mum   Why did you come back?

Dad   I honestly can't remember. If I'd known –

Mum   Why couldn't you have stayed in New York with Paul Robeson and the sharks and left me alone?

Dad   You're the one that pursued me, hen, and you know it. (*To* **Patrick**.) She stole me from Bridget O'Rourke.

Mum   Well, I wish to God I hadn't. I wish to God she was here now, her life in ruins, and I was sitting in her bungalow in Carluke, going to Spain every year.

Dad   You'd never get on the plane.

Mum   I knew twenty years ago I'd made a mistake. We were out with some of his pals and their wives and he was buying a round and I didn't want anything and he said, 'You're having one.' And I said, 'Honestly, I'm fine.' And he said, 'You'll have a gin and bitter lemon. A double. Don't you ever try to drop out of my round again,' and I said, 'Why not? I don't want anything,' and he said, this is in front of everyone, 'I don't care. Drop out of someone else's round. It looks like we're trying to get a round on the cheap. A wife doesn't drop out of her husband's round.' The contempt. I was mortified. I just said, 'Sorry, I never knew that.' But I knew then that I'd made a mistake.

Cath   Before you had me.

Silence.

Dad   I don't remember that.

Mum   Well, I do.

Dad   I knew there was something I hadn't been forgiven for.

Silence.

Mind you, a wife shouldn't drop out of her husband's round.

Mum   Don't make the same mistake I made. Don't throw your life away.

Patrick   I've no intention of –

Mum   I know you as well. 'I want to explore my options, I might go to uni next year, I'll see how I feel.' Next year will turn into the year after, and the year after that, and before you know it you'll be stuck in your hovel in Stonebridge with one of those foul-mouthed little jezebels from the Stag and two screaming babies in filthy nappies.

Patrick   Who are you – Thomas Hardy?

Mum   You think it can't happen to you, but it can.

Patrick   The other night I dreamt I was walking a tightrope over the Niagara Falls and you were screaming, 'If you fall you'll die! It's very high up! Don't fall! You won't survive!' I fell.

Mum   Stonebridge! Why in God's name do you want to live in Stonebridge? What's wrong with your own home?

Patrick   Nothing.

Mum   So what are you doing in bloody Stonebridge?

Patrick   Everybody leaves home sometime. Even if you're brought up in the happiest family in the world . . .

Mum   *Sometime*, not when you've just come back. You couldn't even wait till after your brother's funeral?

Patrick   We didn't know . . . we thought he'd just run away.

Mum   Oh, so that's OK, is it? To leave home when you think your brother's just missing?

No reply.

Well?

Patrick   He wasn't missing when I made the appointment. When I met the guy we thought he'd just gone off for a couple of days to lick his wounds.

Mum   When did you make the appointment?

Patrick   On the Friday. The day before . . . The day Dad went into hospital.

Mum   So you decided to leave home after your father was rushed to hospital?

Patrick   Before.

Mum   Why?

Patrick   I just did.

Mum   You must have had a reason.

Patrick   It doesn't matter now.

Mum   Why?

Patrick   Nothing. Dad and me had a wee run-in.

Mum   What? What happened?

Patrick   Nothing.

Mum (*to* **Dad**)   What happened?

Dad   I haven't the foggiest notion what he's on about. What are you on about?

Patrick   It doesn't matter any more. I'd have left sooner or later, anyway.

Dad   It matters to me.

Mum   It matters to me. What did you do?

Dad   Nothing.

Mum   What did he do?

Patrick   We just had a disagreement. It's over.

Mum   About what?

Dad   That's just what I was wondering.

Patrick   I'm not going to rehash it now. You've done worse. We've got other things to worry about.

Mum   Yes, like you being stuck in Stonebridge for the rest of your life.

Patrick   Like the fact that the undertakers will be here shortly and we've hardly got anything for the sermon. (*To* **Dad**.) Do you never wonder where it went wrong for Johnny?

Mum   Never mind that. You've still got your life ahead of you. Promise me you won't throw it away.

Patrick   I promise I won't throw it away.

Mum   Promise me you won't end up in Stonebridge.

Patrick   There's no chance of me ending up in Stonebridge.

Mum   That's what you think. That's what everyone thinks.

Patrick   I'm telling you, absolutely no chance.

Mum   Do you think I saw myself ending up here?

Patrick   I don't care about that. I will not end up in Stonebridge.

Mum   How do you know?

Patrick   I know.

Mum   No, you don't.

Patrick   Yes, I bloody well do.

Mum   How?

Patrick   I just do.

Mum   How?

Patrick   Because it's horrible. OK? Really . . . horrible.

Cath   I told you.

Patrick   The noise. The stupid boys with their vicious dogs. Piles of shit everywhere.

Mum   Charming.

Patrick   Grown men pissing on the stairs.

Mum (*taken aback*)   I see you've picked up the lingo.

Patrick   Yesterday I saw a man walking along with his four-year-old daughter so off his face he was arguing with an imaginary black guy. The wee girl didn't bat an eyelid.

Dad   How do you know he was black?

Patrick   Because he called him a fucking nigger, of course.

Mum   Patrick Conlan!

Patrick   That's how they talk.

Mum   *They* might talk like that –

Patrick (*ploughing straight on*)   I didn't know what to do. What could I do for her? They give their kids crisps on the way to school and the kids drop the empty packets on the ground in front of them and they say absolutely nothing. Adults drop anything they're finished with on the ground. Cans, cigarette packets, the huge cardboard boxes that their huge tellies came in.

Cath   I told you.

Patrick   I was out running a couple of days ago and there was a woman with two kids and a baby in a buggy and the boy dropped a big McDonald's bag on the pavement. I looked at the mother like, 'Aren't you going to say anything?' and she said something and the boy picked it up. I ran round the corner feeling like Captain America, then I started to replay it Did she say, 'Not there, on the side'? Sure enough on my way back the bag had been moved up against the wall. She thought that was the right thing to do. Where do you start with people like that? It's not poverty; they're richer than we've ever been. They can feed their dogs and buy huge bottles of cider and fags and trolleyloads of garbage from Iceland. When did poor people get so fat?

Dad   What about this?

'No wonder you got plastered
And wandered off, alone.
Your father is a bastard
And your mother is a stone.'

Cath   Right, pack it in, you.

Dad   What, do my thoughts not matter then?

Cath   It's not very helpful.

Dad   My first-born son is being put in the ground tomorrow morning, who should I be helping? I remember him taking his first steps right there.

He indicates the rug in front of the electric fire.

He bends over with his hands to his head and quietly breaks down.

Silence.

He gathers himself and sits up.

Silence.

(*A genuine question.*) How did we end up here?

Mum   I don't know.

Silence.

By mistake.

Dad   I'll say one thing for Johnny, you can write this down, he might not have had the gumption to get away, but he was never going to carry a hod for *anybody*. Unlike muggins here, sweating blood to fill another man's pockets. Maybe he knew the game was up. He was a clever boy. You either exploit or you're exploited. Maybe he realised his best years were behind him and he didn't fancy ploughing on.

Mum   Don't you dare. He was twenty-two! He had no idea what he was doing.

Dad   If you say so.

Mum   Nobody knew it was going to snow.

Dad   It was awful cold.

Mum   The cold doesn't make you invisible. He was right out in the open when he lay down. If it had just been cold you'd have been able to see him from a hundred yards away. He didn't know it was going to snow. He didn't know it would lie for four days. He had no idea what he was doing.

Cath (*to* **Patrick**)   Do you think he killed himself?

Mum   No!

Patrick   I don't think he cared much, either way.

Mum   Rubbish.

Patrick   He told me. He was stuck. He liked smoking and drinking in the pub but he didn't like working. He should have been a toff. He'd've been all right in the House of Lords. He was born into the wrong family.

Cath   I'll never forgive myself.

Patrick   It wasn't your fault.

Cath   You don't think he felt humiliated?

Patrick   Maybe, but he did it to himself. We were only trying to help him. He was probably more upset about not being number one any more. I don't think he was looking forward to anything. He didn't want to end up . . .

Dad   Like me. You can say it. Neither did I.

Cath   We shouldn't have let him do it.

Patrick   He didn't need permission. He was our big brother.

Cath   You don't feel any guilt at all?

Patrick   I'm sorry for lying to him.

Cath   Is that it? What about thinking you were better than him? Letting him *see* that you thought you were better than him?

Patrick   Johnny didn't need me to tell him he'd made a mess of things. It's not my fault if I'm . . . better equipped.

Cath   No, it's your good luck.

Patrick   Fine. It's all luck. His sister died. He was tired. It snowed. He wasn't born into money. His parents couldn't help him.

Mum   So it's our fault.

Patrick   No. You didn't have the money.

Cath   You had the money, Pat.

Patrick   And I came across.

Cath   After you put him through the wringer. He might have deserved it, but that doesn't mean he could cope with it.

Patrick   It was his idea. It's not my fault.

Mum   It's nobody's fault! It was an accident! I don't want to hear another word about it. I'm going for a cigarette. Not another word. I mean it.

She leaves.

Cath   I'm not saying it's your fault. Just that you underestimated how hard life was for him. Like you underestimated how hard it is in Stonebridge.

Patrick *takes this in.*

Cath   I take it you won't be staying there.

Patrick   No.

Cath   And when were you planning on telling me?

Patrick   Sorry. I've been all over the place. I couldn't get to sleep till half five this morning then some moron woke me up at seven tooting his fucking horn.

Cath   So much for 'Time of the Spirit'.

Silence.

Patrick   I'll find somewhere better. Maybe Glasgow.

Cath   What with?

Patrick   Frankie Fisher gave me the four hundred back.

Cath   How come?

Patrick   He asked wee Higgy to pass it on.

Cath   Jesus. Even Frankie Fisher feels guilty. Maybe there's hope for all of us. Even the fat and foul-mouthed and stupid. I eat crisps and smoke and drink big bottles of cider from Iceland. And what's wrong with working in Comet?

Patrick   There's nothing wrong with it. Just not Johnny.

Cath   We can't all be priests and teachers and bloody useless dermatologists. Who'd empty the bins and fight the wars and make the . . . fucking . . . sausages? You were rescued. And you think you're better than the people that were left behind. You think you can save us. Well, you've given up on the starving Africans and you didn't do Johnny much good and you're not going to save me.

Patrick   I'm sorry. I don't think . . . I wasn't . . .

Dad   When you're young and good-looking it doesn't matter if you're poor. Once you stop turning heads you're invisible. If you haven't got money or power nobody will give you the time of day. You might as well be dead.

Cath   Ruth was smoked, Johnny was frozen, what will I be – pickled? Dried! (*Re her skin.*) I'm drying to death.

Mum *enters.*

Mum   They're here.

Nobody knows what to do.

Cath   Christ Almighty. Somebody say something.

Nobody does.

Say a prayer, somebody. They're about to close that coffin for ever.

Silence.

Pat.

Mum   How can an atheist say a prayer?

Patrick   I can say a prayer.

Mum   You've got to mean it.

Patrick   I can do that, too.

Cath   Well do it. Hurry up.

Patrick *goes to the coffin. He looks skyward.*

Patrick   Eh . . .

He waits for the spirit to descend.

Oh God. (*As in the expression of frustration.*)
Oh God, we pray you're there.
We pray you're there.
We pray that Johnny is with you.
And that Ruth is with him.
We want to see Ruth and Johnny again in Heaven.
It is childish. But it could happen.
Better people than me have believed it.

We understand that even if you're there, it doesn't mean that
we go on for ever. Jews manage to believe in you without getting
in a state about the hereafter. Forgive us our self-importance.
Not Johnny. Johnny was self-unimportant, unfortunately.

I'd like to apologise to you, Johnny.
For not lending you the money straight away.
And for lying to you.
For not being more concerned with your safety.
And for looking down on you.
Most of all for looking down on you.
I hope you heard that.

We pray for all the children that have been lost.
And for their parents.

We hope that you are watching over us.
And that pain and sorrow have a purpose.
And will be washed away.

Who wouldn't want that to be true?

A knock.

Cath   Amen. I'll let them in.

Lights.

Methuen Drama Student Editions

Jean Anouilh *Antigone* • John Arden *Serjeant Musgrave's Dance*
Alan Ayckbourn *Confusions* • Aphra Behn *The Rover*
Edward Bond *Lear* • Bertolt Brecht *The Caucasian Chalk Circle*
Life of Galileo • *Mother Courage and her Children*
The Resistible Rise of Arturo Ui • *The Threepenny Opera*
Anton Chekhov *The Cherry Orchard* • *The Seagull* • *Three Sisters*
Uncle Vanya • Caryl Churchill *Serious Money* • *Top Girls*
Shelagh Delaney *A Taste of Honey* • Euripides *Elektra* • *Medea*
Dario Fo *Accidental Death of an Anarchist* • Michael Frayn *Copenhagen*
John Galsworthy *Strife* • Nikolai Gogol *The Government Inspector*
Robert Holman *Across Oka* • Henrik Ibsen *A Doll's House* • *Ghosts*
Hedda Gabler • Charlotte Keatley *My Mother Said I Never Should*
Bernard Kops *Dreams of Anne Frank* • Federico García Lorca
Blood Wedding • *Doña Rosita the Spinster* (bilingual edition) • *The House
of Bernarda Alba* • (bilingual edition) • *Yerma* (bilingual edition) • David
Mamet *Glengarry Glen Ross* • *Oleanna* • Patrick Marber *Closer* • John
Marston *The Malcontent* • Joe Orton *Loot* • Luigi Pirandello *Six
Characters in Search of an Author* • Mark Ravenhill *Shopping and
F***ing* • Willy Russell *Blood Brothers* • *Educating Rita* • Sophocles
Antigone • *Oedipus the King* • Wole Soyinka *Death and the King's
Horseman* • August Strindberg *Miss Julie* • J. M. Synge *The Playboy
of the Western World* • Theatre Workshop *Oh What a Lovely War*
Timberlake Wertenbaker *Our Country's Good* • Arnold Wesker *The
Merchant* • Oscar Wilde *The Importance of Being Earnest* • Tennessee
Williams *A Streetcar Named Desire* • *The Glass Menagerie*

Methuen Drama Modern Plays
include work by

Edward Albee
Jean Anouilh
John Arden
Margaretta D'Arcy
Peter Barnes
Sebastian Barry
Brendan Behan
Dermot Bolger
Edward Bond
Bertolt Brecht
Howard Brenton
Anthony Burgess
Simon Burke
Jim Cartwright
Caryl Churchill
Noël Coward
Lucinda Coxon
Sarah Daniels
Nick Darke
Nick Dear
Shelagh Delaney
David Edgar
David Eldridge
Dario Fo
Michael Frayn
John Godber
Paul Godfrey
David Greig
John Guare
Peter Handke
David Harrower
Jonathan Harvey
Iain Heggie
Declan Hughes
Terry Johnson
Sarah Kane
Charlotte Keatley
Barrie Keeffe
Howard Korder

Robert Lepage
Doug Lucie
Martin McDonagh
John McGrath
Terrence McNally
David Mamet
Patrick Marber
Arthur Miller
Mtwa, Ngema & Simon
Tom Murphy
Phyllis Nagy
Peter Nichols
Sean O'Brien
Joseph O'Connor
Joe Orton
Louise Page
Joe Penhall
Luigi Pirandello
Stephen Poliakoff
Franca Rame
Mark Ravenhill
Philip Ridley
Reginald Rose
Willy Russell
Jean-Paul Sartre
Sam Shepard
Wole Soyinka
Simon Stephens
Shelagh Stephenson
Peter Straughan
C. P. Taylor
Theatre de Complicite
Theatre Workshop
Sue Townsend
Judy Upton
Timberlake Wertenbaker
Roy Williams
Snoo Wilson
Victoria Wood

Printed in the United Kingdom
by Lightning Source UK Ltd.
134619UK00001B/100-276/P

9 781408 113882